Interface

Delron Shirley

2013

Cover design by Jeremy Shirley

Table of Contents

To obtain permission to quote material from this book contact:

Delron Shirley
3210 Cathedral Spires Dr.
Colorado Springs, CO 80904
teachallnations@msn.com

Introduction

While I was ministering in Belfast, Ireland, my host took me around the city to become acquainted a bit with its history and traditions. We, of course, made a stop at the shipyard where the ill-fated Titanic was built and made an extensive tour of sites where the bloody conflict between the city's Protestant and Catholic populations had played out. Finally, we found one bright spot in our expedition through the city that had suffered so much pain and agony over the years. We came upon the community where C. S. Lewis had lived and discovered that they had erected a simple, yet impactful, memorial to his life and accomplishments. The life-size statue of the author, philosopher, and theologian depicted him looking into the wardrobe that became so famous in his <u>Chronicles</u> <u>of</u> <u>Narnia</u> series. It was by crawling into this wardrobe that the four Pevensie children were magically transported into the kingdom of Narnia where they met Aslan, the Great Lion, Lewis' allegory for Jesus. This magical wardrobe was depicted as actually connecting the temporal dimension of earth with the supernatural realm where the kingdom of heaven could be literally encountered as it conflicted with the demonic dominion. To those four young siblings, that wardrobe was an interface between two worlds – between reality and the symbolic kingdom of Narnia.

Not long after my visit to Belfast, I began to randomly hear the word "interface." Sometimes, I would pick up the word in a conversation or in something I was reading. But most often, the word would simply pop into my head for no apparent reason. This unusual emphasis on a seemingly random thought reminded me of a similar experience many years before when the word "Africa" suddenly started popping into my head. At that time, the closest I had ever been to Africa was Busch Garden's Dark Continent theme park in

Tampa, Floria. As I kept encountering this single word over and over with no explanation as to what it could possibly mean to me, I began to have more and more interaction with Africans. The college where I served as dean suddenly began to receive an influx of African students. In fact, at one point, there were more Africans than American students. Then, I began to receive invitations to minister in Africa, a trend that continues to this day with at least one or two trips to Africa every year. So, I knew that this repeated impression of the word "Africa" was a communication from God. But what could the similar experience with the word "interface" mean?

An interface is the interaction point, or sometimes a collision point, between two different systems. We use the term most often in discussing the meshing together of two different computer components – sometimes the linking of two different software systems and sometimes the linking of a software system with the computer's hardware system. The term is also used in meteorology to speak of the point where two different weather patterns meet, usually resulting in dramatic – or even violent – acts of nature. "Interface" may also find its way into discussions of interpersonal relationships as we try to bring people with different cultures, political or social viewpoints, or philosophies "to the table" and get them "on the same page." Physically, we live in a world of interfaces. Every time we look out a window or open a door, we experience an interface. We may be sitting in a toasty warm den next to a roaring blaze in the fireplace, while a blizzard is raging just outside our window. That window is the interface between two radically different worlds.

Not long ago, I experienced a very powerful demonstration of such an interface in the country of Nigeria. I had arrived after a very long day of travel to find that the first event on my schedule was an all-night prayer vigil. Well, that was the first time in my life that I was glad to be experiencing jet lag; my body felt like it was still day, even though it was nighttime in Africa. After making it through the night of prayer, I went to the hotel and drew the thick curtains shut

2

before going to bed. When I woke up in the pitch-black room, the clock on my nightstand read three o'clock. Because it was totally dark I assumed that it was 3 AM, but then I remembered that I had still been at the church at 3 AM. When I opened the curtains, the brilliant African sun came blazing into my room assuring me that it was 3 PM! That window was an interface between the artificially dark world inside my room and the reality of the sunlit world outside.

In the Bahamas, we learned a little song that illustrates that there are also interfaces between spiritual kingdoms:

Shut de do; keep out de debil, debil!
Shut de do; keep de debil in de ni-eet!

So, it was with all these thoughts racing through my mind that I set out on a scriptural quest to understand the spiritual significance of interfaces. From this quest was born this series of short studies.

This book should be viewed as an anthology because each of the seven studies was written at a different time with no deliberate connection to the other six. However, there is a thread running through these independent studies that ties them all together as they communicate different aspects of one unified message – being strategic in our spirituality. The first study deals directly with the interfaces discussed in the Bible where we connect with the world around us, the kingdom of heaven, and the kingdom of darkness. The second study in the series discusses finding the sensitive balance between two necessary interfaces – our need to spend time with God and our mandate to rise up and interact with the world. The third and fourth studies have to do with the biblical truths that we need to understand in order to accurately interface with our God, our world, and ourselves. In the letters to the seven churches of Asia Minor recorded in Revelation chapters two and three, only one of the churches is specifically mentioned as being at an interface; the church at Philadelphia is said to have an open door set before it. Interestingly, this is also the only church

3

that is specifically mentioned as having a relationship with the Word of God. (Revelation 3:8, 3:10) Therefore, it is significant that we take some time to explore some foundational, biblical truths that we must stand upon as we approach the various interfaces set before us. The fifth study takes us through the life of one of our most beloved biblical heroes – David, the shepherd boy who killed a giant and wrote beautiful psalms. Although his life was riddled with one failure after another, he somehow attained the report that he was a man after God's own heart, which is the key to opening the doors of interface with the world that we learn about in the letter to the Philadelphian church. (Revelation 3:7) Next, we look at what it really means to have a heart after the very heart of God – one that Bob Pierce, founder of World Vision, described as being broken with the same things that break the heart of God. Finally, the book concludes with a challenge to never fall short of the opportunities and blessings that God has provided for us as we interface with the One who sent us and those with whom we are to interface.

Chapter One
Doors, Windows, and Gates

When I began my study of interfaces in the Bible, I saw immediately that throughout the Bible, doors were depicted as the interface point between two spiritual dimensions. As early as the fourth chapter of the Bible, God spoke of a door that determined the spiritual destiny of one of the first members of the human family. When Cain killed Abel, the Lord warned him that sin was crouching at his very door. (Genesis 4:7) Just a bit further into the saga of the household of mankind, God made a decision to destroy the human race because of their rebelliousness. At that point, He commanded the one remaining righteous representative of the family to build an ark so that life could be preserved on the planet. Explicitly delineated in the plan for this vessel was the provision for a door (Genesis 6:16), which was later shut once all the animals and people that were to be saved were inside (Genesis 7:16). That door was an interface between salvation and judgment. Later on, two cities came to God's attention because of their extreme wickedness. When He sent two angels to rescue the one righteous family within these doomed municipalities, the perverted men of the region attacked the celestial visitors, desiring to have homosexual relationships with them. When Lot tried to convince the vile men to abandon their horrific plan, the mob grew even more incensed, until one of the angels had to reach outside and jerk his host to safety inside the house. When he shut the door, it became an interface between the seething hotbed of perversion outside and the heavenly presence of the peace of God inside. (Genesis 19:10) When God delivered the Israelites after four hundred years of bondage in Egypt, He sent one last plague upon the captors to convince them that the chosen people must be freed – a death angel that was to enter every home and claim the firstborn of the family. However, a provision was made for the people of God; the blood of the Passover lamb was to be spread on the door as an indication that the household was dedicated to God.

The bloodstained door was an interface between life and death, keeping out the death angel and giving life to those inside. (Exodus 12:22)

As I continued to study the doors in the Bible, I soon discovered that many significant acts in the Old Testament were often done at the door. The priests were sanctified at the door of the tabernacle. (Exodus 29:4) Sacrifices were made at the door of the tabernacle. (Exodus 29:11) The people worshiped at the doors of their own tents. (Exodus 33:10) Bond slaves had their ears pierced at the doorway to indicate that they had decided to remain in servitude to their kind masters, even though they were technically able to go free. (Deuteronomy 15:17) Immoral daughters were stoned at the doors of their fathers' homes. (Deuteronomy 22:21) The apparent reason for all such activities being held at the doorway was that these portals were seen as interfaces between the physical and spiritual realms. Therefore, acts done there symbolized to the spiritual world what was being done in the physical and, at the same time, notified the physical realm about what had transpired in the spiritual dimension. Probably, the ultimate expression of this concept of the spiritual-physical interface is seen in the door that was opened in heaven that allowed John the Revelator to see the very throne of God and gain a vision of the end time. (Revelation 4:1)

Jesus personalized the message of the interface when He said, *I am the door for the sheep.* (John 10:7, 10:9) When He made this statement, He was referring to the practice of the shepherds of His time who would gather their sheep in the sheepfold for the night. Since there was no gate to close the opening through which the sheep entered, the shepherd would actually lie on the ground in the opening as a defense against predators that would try to attack the sheep during the night. In the morning, he would get up and take the sheep out of the enclosure to find food and water. He personally became the interface between the sheep and their enemies at night and the interface between the sheep and their provisions during the day. Jesus also taught us parables that helped us understand

6

that we are all living at the interface between the realities of heaven and our ordinary lives, when He said that the heavenly kingdom was at the door (Matthew 24:33); however, He explained in the very next chapter that some would fail to enter the kingdom of heaven before the door – the interface – was closed. (Matthew 25:10)

But the most timely message about doors in the Bible seems to be the fact that God has given us open doors into the world around us. He wants us to understand that He has provided opportunities for us to interface with the world we live in in order to bring men and women into His kingdom and to bring His kingdom into their lives. In the book of Revelation, He wrote to the church at Philadelphia, *I have set before thee an open door, and no man can shut it.* (verse 3:8) Paul also spoke of the fact that God had set before him open doors through which he could take the gospel to the world:

> *For a great door and effectual is opened unto me, and there are many adversaries.* (I Corinthians 16:9)
> *Furthermore, when I came to Troas to preach Christ's gospel, and a door was opened unto me of the Lord.* (II Corinthians 2:12)
> *Withal praying also for us, that God would open unto us a door of utterance, to speak the mystery of Christ, for which I am also in bonds.* (Colossians 4:3)

There is no such thing as a closed door for the church. Jesus would not have told us to go to all the nations if we weren't going to be able to get in. (Matthew 28:19) He would not have told us to preach the gospel to every creature in all the world if we were not going to be able to get to all of them. (Mark 16:15) Even though we often speak of specific people and even whole nations as being closed to the gospel, the scriptural truth is that there is no such thing as a closed door.

A very dear friend of mine in the country of Nepal had a desire to present the gospel to his countrymen; however, the country was considered "closed" because the Hindu government had outlawed any form of Christian evangelism under the country's anti-proselytizing laws. However, knowing that God would not have given him the desire unless He would also give him the means (Philippians 2:13), he prayed until he came up with a creative idea (Proverbs 8:12). Since many people in the country were dying from diseases that were being spread by poor hygiene and ignorance of some very simple sanitation practices, he knew that the government would approve of a privately funded health initiative to assist the people. So he produced a brochure that gave some very simple steps to better hygiene and proper sanitation; however, he added one unexpected chapter. Since sin is the worst pollutant of all (Numbers 18:32), he included a chapter on the only way to eradicate this contaminant – salvation through Jesus Christ. As was required by the national authorities, this piece of literature had to be approved by the government before it could be printed and distributed in the country. Apparently, the official who reviewed the pamphlet didn't read it through to the very end and gave it the authoritative stamp! Soon my friend, with all necessary governmental approval, launched a campaign to canvass every house and hut in every city and village in the nation. Before long, Nepal experienced an unprecedented move toward God, and the church in this country became the fastest growing segment in the entire Body of Christ – in what was considered to be a nation whose doors were "closed to the gospel."

In one Islamic nation that has been devastated by seemingly unending war, the government decided that they needed to take a census to determine the full impact of the war on their citizenry. They felt that there needed to be an accurate accounting of the number of men who had lost their eyesight or limbs and the number of families who had lost sons, fathers, or husbands in the fighting. To implement such a thorough study, they needed to employ an outside agency that was trained and equipped to do such a door-to-door canvass. By divine plan, there was a group of Christians in that very nation who were praying for an "open door" to share their faith in this "closed" Muslim environment. They answered the government's call for a third-party census organization with the response that they were part of an organization that did extensive door-to-door visitation around the world and that they were uniquely trained and equipped for just such a task. Before long, they were given governmental approval and backing to begin visiting every home in the country to take the government-sanctioned survey. Once the interviewees completed the questionnaire, the census takers suggested that they would like to thank the family for their time by leaving behind a small gift as a token of their appreciation for providing the necessary information. That gift, of course, was a copy of the Arabic New Testament, the Jesus Film in the local language, or another simple gospel message. All this in a "closed" nation! Why? Because there is no such thing as a closed door when God has said that He has set before us an open door!

I was recently in the nation of Trinidad and Tobago as part of a team helping train the local Christians in door-to-door evangelism. As we rode the bus to our designated canvass site, we prayed that God would grant us:

Open doors to spread the gospel according to Colossians 4:2-3 NIV, *Devote yourselves to prayer, being watchful and thankful. And pray for us, too, that God may open a door for our message, so that we may proclaim the mystery of Christ, for which I am in chains.*

Open minds to hear the gospel according to Acts 26:17-18 NIV, *I will rescue you from your own people and from the Gentiles. I am sending you to them to open their eyes and turn them from darkness to light, and from the power of Satan to God, so that they may receive forgiveness of sins and a place among those who are sanctified by faith in me.*

Open hearts to embrace the gospel according to II Corinthians 4:6 NIV, *For God, who said, "Let light*

9

shine out of darkness," made his light shine in our hearts to give us the light of the knowledge of God's glory displayed in the face of Christ.

Open heavens to reveal the gospel according to Isaiah 45:8 NLT, *Open up, O heavens, and pour out your righteousness. Let the earth open wide so salvation and righteousness can sprout up together. I, the Lord, created them.*

After the prayers, we found the people to be very receptive to the gospel. On two specific days of our outreach, every individual we visited – and even whole families – responded to the salvation message. In one street corner, I came upon a group of young men standing with money in their hands, apparently waiting for a drug deal. As I shared the gospel with them, they all responded positively and prayed the sinner's prayer while still holding their drug money in their hands. At one home, a young man received the Lord after the presentation of the gospel using a bracelet made of colored beads that illustrate the plan of salvation. As an afterthought while the team was walking away from the young man's home, one of the ladies in the team turned back and asked if he would like to have a couple bracelets to share with his friends. After crossing the street to share with a family there, the team crossed back to visit the gentleman's next-door neighbor. When the man in the house came to the door, he was already wearing one of the beaded bracelets. The new convert had already been to his home and shared the gospel with him! All this happened in a predominately Hindu region where closed doors had been opened by faith, prayer, and courage to go share the gospel!

Another significant interface in the Bible is the window. Throughout the Bible, we see windows as the interface with heaven that allows the supernatural to invade the natural realm. The flood during Noah's day came as a result of the windows of heaven being open. (Genesis 7:11) Rahab and her family were saved because she hung a cord out of her window. (Joshua 2:15) That window was her key to avoiding the destruction that everyone else in Jericho experienced as well as the key to the deliverance that awaited only the one family with an interface to salvation. When Samaria was under siege and the blockade had cut them off from all sources of supplies to the point where they were suffering famine so severe that women were eating their own babies, the prophet declared that bread would sell for pennies within twenty-four hours. The king's chief advisor retorted with the exclamation that such a thing could not happen even if God opened heaven's windows. God did miraculously provide, and the people had all the food and supplies that they could ever have asked for when the windows of heaven did open. (II Kings 7:2) Although it is not specifically said that there were windows opened, Psalm 78:24 tells us that it was the raining down of manna from heaven that sustained the children of Israel for forty years as they wandered through the barren desert – their interface between starvation and provision. Daniel prayed at an open window, and God saved him from the mouths of the lions. (Daniel 6:10) Elisha directed King Joash to open a window and shoot arrows through that open portal as symbols of the Lord's deliverance from their enemy Syria. (II Kings 13:17)

But God doesn't stop with these historic events; He goes on to make a perpetual promise to His people that He will provide them with open windows – an interface with His blessing.

> *Bring ye all the tithes into the storehouse,*
> *that there may be meat in mine house, and*
> *prove me now herewith, saith the LORD of*
> *hosts, if I will not open you the windows of*
> *heaven, and pour you out a blessing, that*
> *there shall not be room enough to receive it.*
> (Malachi 3:10)

A number of years ago, my wife and I arrived in the island nation of Sri Lanka to minister in a youth camp that had been arranged for the Christian high school and college students in that Buddhist country. When our host picked us up at the airport, he announced that we were going to have to cancel the retreat. He then went on to explain that the country was encountering severe drought and that there was no water in the cisterns at the retreat center. Without water for cooking, cleaning, and washing, it would be impossible to house the group at the camp. I explained that we had spent a lot of money in advance to cover the camp expenses and had flown all the way from America for the event. In my mind, it was impossible to cancel the retreat. There had to be a way to make it work. I asked for just twenty-four hours before he made his final decision. That night, we asked the Lord for the windows of heaven to be opened in some miraculous way, and God answered our prayer in an even more dramatic way than I had anticipated. (Ephesians 3:20) We had the most horrendous rainstorm I have ever experienced. It didn't just "rain cats and dogs"; it was more like lions and wolves. I had never seen anything like it; the rain came down by the buckets full – no, barrels full. Not only did the cisterns fill to overflowing, the draught that was crippling the nation's agriculture was immediately alleviated. As a result, we were able to go forward with our plans for the retreat where we saw many young lives changed and destinies set. It wasn't until I revisited the nation almost thirty years later and was asked by one of the prominent pastors of the country to preach in his church that I saw proof of the remaining effect of the night that the windows of heaven were opened. That pastor, who is now a significant leader in the country, was called into the ministry as a high school student in that camp that would have been canceled had God not opened the windows of heaven.

Open windows can come in many different shapes and sizes. The challenge to increase our faith to the next level came during one of our annual church conventions when I felt directed to make a five-hundred-dollar donation to help our church's humanitarian program. Not having that much cash in the bank account at the moment, I made the gift on a credit card that would give me about a month to believe for the extra finances to come in. When I took that step of faith, God proved to me that money does indeed grow on trees. In our backyard, we had a giant walnut tree whose upper limbs brushed the very heavens. It was the home of a multitude of gray squirrels that scampered up and down its trunk and ducked into its hollow knotholes only to reappear on the other side of the tree ten feet further down the trunk. This disappearance and reappearance of the furry little creatures became a little discomforting to us, since it meant that the tree must be hollow for some major section of its trunk. Since the tree leaned across the roof of our home, we began to feel that it would endanger our home and our lives if it were to ever be blown over. Several severe storms took their toll of limbs from other trees in our yard; yet the giant walnut remained intact even though it rocked and creaked with the violent winds. I talked to several companies about removing the tree but was constantly offered bids that were far beyond my price range. One friend of mine who did tree removal as a sideline volunteered to take it down for us as a favor. But, after climbing the tree and surveying how much actually reached over the house, he descended and rescinded. We tried to postpone the removal until a later date when we might have the extra cash to pay for the service, but a violent windstorm raged through our area bringing down one of the trees in our yard. My wife insisted that we act immediately before the next storm razed the walnut tree that, in turn, would crush our home. Since the next week was the annual convention and I knew that I would be busy morning, noon, and night, I promised that – without fail – I would call in a tree company immediately after the conference. One day during the conference, I came home at lunchtime and found a stranger standing in my backyard. I went to find out what he wanted and was greeted with a proposal that I sell him the walnut lumber from the tree. He had been in the area for some other wood procurement and had spotted this tree towering on the skyline. It seemed ideal for his veneer business and he was willing to pay five hundred dollars for it! Of course, I quickly settled the deal and paid off the charge for our faith gift. Not only did God honor our faith, He gave us free removal of the tree that would have cost us several hundred dollars otherwise. God opened a window with that walnut tree that allowed me to help the poor around the world and to also take care of a personal need.

When I was a "poor college student," I had to carefully ration my funds. One Friday night, I was at a special missionary meeting at church when I felt the Lord's prompting to give all the money I had in the missions offering. Doing so meant that I would be totally "broke" for the next two weeks. It was a real step of faith to do so, but I decided to give the money and believe God that He would honor His promise to open the windows of heaven and pour out a blessing upon me. When I got back to the dorm that night, there was a note on my door that I needed to call one of the professors <u>that</u> night, no matter how late it was. It was really strange that there was such urgency in the message, so I made the call – even though it was pushing midnight. It turned out that the professor had received a business opportunity for the following day and needed an assistant to go with him. He wanted me to work with him on the project and promised to pay me on the spot. Wow, within hours of "putting the Lord to the test with my giving," He had indeed opened the windows of heaven. Not only did I work that following day and not only did I get back more than I had given to the missionary, the job turned into an ongoing opportunity that gave me pocket money for many months to come. There was a door of opportunity to bless the work of the Lord through the missionary, but it also took the windows of heaven to make it possible for me to do so.

When our church was planning a mission trip to the Philippines, I felt a real desire to be part of the team, but there was no way I could afford it. We had no extra cash and what extra money I could collect needed to go to pay back a loan that I had taken from my father-in-law. One of the elders at the church knew of my desire to be part of the team and volunteered to pray with me about it. His prayer was that God would open the windows of heaven and make a way for me to go through the door of opportunity that stood before me. To be honest, I didn't anticipate much and went on with my life, with one of my primary objectives being to settle my debts. When I

14

collected enough money to pay back the loan my father-in-law had extended to me, I took the cash to my mother-in-law because my father-in-law had recently died. To my amazement, she responded, "That was between you and him, not between us. You don't need to pay me." The debt was canceled, and I was left with the exact amount of cash necessary to pay for my ticket for the mission. Where there are open doors, there are also open windows!

Can you bear just one more story? Early one year, I began to have a deep sensation that I should plan to join our ministry's Holy Land tour that year. Since the trip wasn't until November, I knew that I had plenty of time to make the arrangements, but there was one major hurdle in my path – the money. At that particular time in my life, our family budget was stretched to the max, and there was no way I could ever expect to add in the cost of a trip to Israel. As each day went by, I was more and more stirred in my spirit that I was supposed to be on that trip. I somehow felt that it was a divine appointment. But as each day passed, it was also more and more evident that I could not afford to go. I couldn't see any way to squeeze any more outgo into the budget without a new source of income. Then came the call from a pastor friend of mine asking me if I could fill his pulpit one Sunday while he was going to be out of town. Immediately, I thought of my need for some extra income and thought that this must be God's way of providing it. If I went out as a guest speaker in a few churches during the year, I could likely get enough honorariums to cover the cost of the trip to Israel. Since I had my own responsibilities at my home church, I told my friend that I'd call him back once I checked with my pastor. To my chagrin, my pastor's answer was, "No, I need you here!" All I was scheduled to do was to make announcements – a job that certainly didn't seem to warrant preempting my opportunity to go out to preach. However, I submissively called my friend and told him that I would have to decline his offer. Well, the weeks passed; and as time for the tour drew closer, I was sure that the plane would be taking off without me. That is until the day I was called into the office of the tour director. The lady

15

who was scheduled to host the tour was pregnant, and her doctor had insisted that she not fly due to some complications that were developing. An alternative host had to be selected, and my name was on the short list. Since I was a Bible college teacher, I was certainly qualified to answer any questions the tour members would have. Plus, I had been to Israel as part of my seminary training, so I was at least a bit familiar with the sites that we would be visiting. As you might well guess, it only took a nanosecond for me to accept the offer. Apparently, I did a pretty good job because I was invited back as the tour host for the next several years and given opportunities to visit Rome and Egypt, as well as make numerous trips to the Holy Land. Open windows make for open doors!

So far, I've been talking about the financial aspect of open windows, but there is one more incident of the interface between heaven and earth that I'd like to consider. It is recorded in Matthew 3:16 where Jesus was anointed when heaven was opened and the Holy Spirit came upon Him in the form of a dove. Even though the passage does not specifically mention a window, we can visualize that the portal through which the dove descended must have been a window, or at least a window-like opening. This story introduced a new significance to the interface between heaven and earth. It is not only physical things such as food and financial blessing that we can anticipate when we interface with heaven at its open windows. There are also spiritual empowerments awaiting us at this interface. In order for us to be able to go through all the open doors that are set before us, we need the open windows of spiritual anointing as well as the open windows of finances.

After hearing all the excuses of the Old Testament characters (Gideon said that he couldn't really be a mighty man of valor because of his family background; Jeremiah countered that he couldn't be a prophet to the nations because he was too young; Isaiah objected that he couldn't speak for the Lord because his lips were unclean; Moses retorted that there was no way he could present himself before Pharaoh because he stuttered; ten of the spies that Moses sent into the Promise

Land said that it would be impossible to possess the land because they were "grasshoppers," and the list goes on), God must have been fed up with flimsy human excuses by the time that the New Testament rolled around. Therefore, when Jesus gave His Great Commission, He didn't pause long enough for the disciples to interject their objections. When He told the disciples in Matthew that they were to go disciple all nations, He didn't take a breath before adding, *and, lo, I am with you alway, even unto the end of the world.* (verse 28:20) In Mark's version, He told them to preach the gospel to every creature, but didn't give them a second to interrupt before He also promised that miraculous signs would follow them as they went out to do so. (verses 16:17-18) When Luke recorded His directive that the disciples were to be witnesses among all nations, he reported that Jesus kept right on talking as He told them to go to Jerusalem where they were to wait until they received supernatural power from on high. (verse 24:49) John's rendition of the Great Commission records that Jesus punctuated His statement to the disciples that He was sending them out the same way His Father had sent Him by breathing on them and commanding them to receive the Holy Spirit. (verse 20:22) Acts reports the final words of Jesus at yet another giving of the Great Commission. Again, Jesus didn't leave an "out" for the disciples in that He insisted that they would receive power when the Holy Ghost came upon them so that they would be able to be witnesses in Jerusalem, Judea, Samaria, and unto the uttermost parts of the earth. (Acts 1:8)

I'd like to illustrate this principle with a couple stories from the subcontinent of India. The first comes from the central part of the country near the city of Nagpur where there are many temples dedicated to the worship of the cobra deity. One of the graduates of the Bible college where I taught was preaching in the villages in that area but was experiencing serious opposition from the local people. That is until one particular night after a fairly strong downpour. Since the ground was muddy, he didn't think much about the fact that it seemed that the ground was moving under his feet. It was probably just the mud shifting under his weight. That is until he saw how all the villagers suddenly seemed spellbound by his message and were clinging to every word he was saying. Since it seemed that their eyes were fixed on his feet, he looked down to find out what had captivated them so. It was then that he realized that the movement was not just mud; it was a giant king cobra! He was standing square on the back of one of the most venomous snakes in the world, and it was not even attempting to strike him. He continued preaching and gave the altar call at which the entire village responded and received salvation. Once he stepped off the serpent's back, it calmly slithered into the bush. The news about this preacher who had authority over their cobra god (Luke 10:19) quickly spread to every village in the area, and the villagers welcomed him, his message, and his Savior! The second illustration is set in a remote village in Tamil Nadu State in southern India. A little white-haired Indian man had been trying year after year to evangelize his Hindu village for Christ. Yet, the people's hearts and ears were closed. Finally, one day at an evangelism training conference in the city of Madras (now known as Chennai), he learned the principle that the Great Commission is accompanied with an open heaven of spiritual anointing that makes it possible to fulfill it. Returning to his village with a new power from his new relationship with the Holy Spirit, he found that an old lady in the village had been gored by a water buffalo. Laying his hands on her, he commanded that she be totally healed. Instantly, her crippled legs received strength and her mangled body was straightened. Since the whole village had seen the woman's condition after the attack and then saw her miraculous recovery, everyone suddenly believed that the old man's message was real. The village that had rejected his testimony year after year was converted overnight.

The flow of supernatural anointing through the open windows of heaven makes it possible for doors of ministry to open before us.

There is one other arena of interface that we must investigate to make our biblical study complete – gates. In the Bible, the gates of a city are symbolic of authority because that is where the elders and decision makers of the city gathered to hold their court and council. (Genesis 19:1; Deuteronomy 16:18, 22:15, 25:7; Ruth 4:11; II Samuel 19:8; Esther 2:21; Proverbs 24:7, 31:23) Gates were also a place of strength, fortification, and defense. (I Chronicles 22:3; Nehemiah 2:17) Although the gates were interfaces between the city and the society outside of the city, they were specifically designed as a barrier to keep the outside influence outside and to protect what was inside. Yes, the gates were open so that commerce and trade could occur, but the positioning of the elders and city leaders at the gate put them in the position to filter out any influence that they did not want to enter their society. Additionally, the fortification of the gate protected the city from the physical intrusion of wild beasts, bandits, and invading armies. Because of the significance of the loss of this protection, it is easy for us to understand why Nehemiah recorded that the king's cupbearer's countenance looked downcast when he heard the report of the fallen gates of his beloved Jerusalem (verse 2:3) and that he considered that his people were living in reproach.

> *Then said I unto them, Ye see the distress that we are in, how Jerusalem lieth waste, and the gates thereof are burned with fire: come, and let us build up the wall of Jerusalem, that we be no more a reproach.*
> (verse 2:17)

It is with this exact idea of the reproach of fallen gates that I'd like to further our study of gates. My focus will be drawn from Jesus' words to His disciples, and Peter in specific, that the gates of hell cannot prevail against His church. (Matthew 16:18) To understand this statement, we need to consider exactly what Jesus must have intended when He referred to the gates of hell. The first suggestion I would like to make is that since there are twelve gates to heaven, or at least the New Jerusalem (Revelation 21:13), perhaps there are also twelve gates of hell. My second thought is that if there really are twelve gates to hell, perhaps these spiritual gates are paralleled by the natural gates that existed in the physical realm of the historical city of Jerusalem. If these thoughts do indeed carry any significance, then it is likely that we can find the specific areas of interface between the church and the strongholds that the devil has set up in human society. When Nehemiah went back to Jerusalem to rid the city of its reproach, he found exactly twelve gates. To me, at least, this is a message of twelve areas where the church needs to aggressively attack strongholds of the enemy and rebuild our positions of authority while tearing down the demonic powers that have set themselves in position there.

The first gate that Nehemiah set out to repair was the gate of the fountain. (verse 2:14) This gate took its name from the fact that it was located next to the Pool of Siloam. Of course, we know this body of water from the story in John chapter nine of the blind man whom Jesus sent to this pool to wash his eyes so that he could receive his sight. The association of this pool, and therefore, the accompanying gate with healing suggests that one area of demonic authority in our society is in the arena of healthcare. It is no secret that the devil wants people sick and that God is in the business of making people well. Jesus healed the sick and sent His disciples out to do the same. (Matthew 4:24, 10:8, 16:18; Mark 1:34; Luke 4:40 10:9; Acts 5:15-16, 10:38, 19:12) Unfortunately, many in the church today have surrendered this gate through denying that God wants to heal people supernaturally, and some have even gone so far as to advocate that ministers who practice "faith healing" are instruments of the devil. In addition, the struggle at the gate of health has extended beyond the arena of supernatural healing into the medical profession. The enemy has taken hold of medical science and the government funds that support it to implement his own diabolical plans. During the days of the conquest of the New World, vast populations of the native inhabitants were decimated because the settlers brought with them diseases that the people isolated on the far side of the earth had no immunities to. Even though these pandemics were totally unplanned and not orchestrated, evil governments today have plans for similar scenarios through planned biological warfare. In addition, our own healthcare system is poised so that the intrusion of some evil power could turn our immunization program into a time bomb that could wipe out our whole population and the future generations. But, leaving aside this futuristic diabolical mass extermination scenario, let's take a look at what is actually happening in the American healthcare system right now. Our present national healthcare system forces students and workers in certain areas to participate in immunization programs, even when there is substantial evidence that the vaccines used may be detrimental to the patient's overall health. Employers are forced to provide birth control benefits (even the morning after pill, which is essentially a form of abortion) to their employees even when such practices violate the employer's religious convictions. Our pro-abortion healthcare system has terminated the lives of more than three hundred times the number of deaths caused by the atomic blast on Hiroshima, ten times the number of deaths in the Nazi death camps, and equal to the total population of the seventy-two largest cities in our country. Stem cell research and the advocacy of euthanasia add to the fortification that the enemy has placed at this gate. Historically, the church has recognized the necessity of confronting the stronghold of disease by establishing church-sponsored hospitals at home and mission hospitals and clinics around the world; however, there is a new need today for the church to aggressively take back the policymaking position in the current healthcare system in our country.

Nehemiah's second gate was the sheep gate. (verse 3:1) This gate was the entrance through which the sheep that were to be sacrificed in the temple were brought into the city. Therefore, it represents religion. I guess the very idea that the church needs to take charge of religion will bring a puzzled grin to most of our faces, but it is true. The enemy has taken advantage of the broken-down gate of religion and turned it into one of his own strongholds. On a recent train ride inside the country of Peru, I had the privilege of sharing a berth with a bishop in one of the nation's major denominations. As we talked about the state of the church in America, the topic of same-sex marriage came up. This particular man was a strong believer in the gospel and stood for biblical principles, yet he described to me the tremendous battles he has had to fight in order to keep his denomination from sanctioning gay marriage and ordination of homosexuals. He confirmed that these issues were reccurring items on the agenda every year at the national convention. He shared with me how vocal the advocates for gay rights are within his denomination and how close they have actually come to making the denomination change its position. When he began to mention names of specific church leaders who were in favor of the gay agenda, I'm sure that he could see my mouth drop. Simply pulling out of the denominational church because of their liberal stance is not the answer. In doing so, we allow the whole system to be fully taken over and give the enemy a place to establish a gate of authority in society. True believers must bombard the stronghold of religion and reestablish it as a gate of heaven rather than a gate of hell.

The third gate in disrepair was the fish gate (verse 3:3), so called because it faced the Sea of Galilee and Jordan River where fishing, one of the most lucrative of Israel's industries, flourished. This gate represents commerce. We often hear references to Jesus and the poor fishermen who traveled with Him. Actually, this is probably the farthest thing from the truth. The fish that were harvested from the Sea of Galilee were considered a delicacy throughout the Roman Empire, and the men employed in the businesses of catching and marketing them became extremely wealthy. In fact, archeologists have excavated the homes of Galilean fishermen in which caches of thousands of gold coins were buried. Peter actually had a fishing company with partners and more than one ship; therefore, he was likely a prosperous businessman. (Luke 5:7) His mother-in-law had a home with a tiled roof (Mark 2:4, Weymouth Translation), indicating that she was from an upper class family. Christians today are called to take positions of authority in the world of commerce. Without an expression of Christian ethics in the business world, the poor will continually be slaves to the rich and powerful, the desires and wishes of the rich will be imposed upon the total populace, and a few wealthy businessmen will buy the votes of our politicians. The gates of commerce must be taken back from hell and returned to the church.

The next gate for reconstruction was the old gate. (verse 3:6) To me, this gate speaks of the media, entertainment, and sports. I would love to see the grimaces on the faces of most of my readers right now, but let me give just a few lines to explain. The scriptures repeatedly speak of the old man and the old mentality. (II Corinthians 5:17, Ephesians 4:22, Colossians 3:9) The old mentality is communicated and established through what we see and hear (Luke 8:18), and we are most vulnerable to outside influences through the media, entertainment, and sports. Therefore, the old way of thinking can readily be associated with these three areas of communication. How do we make a decision about what politician to vote for? The messages we get through the media. What hairstyle do we decide to adopt? The one we see on our favorite entertainer. What deodorant do we use? The one promoted by our favorite sports figure. After all, there is a reason we call these people "idols." In addition, this gate was repaired by Joiada whose name means "Jehovah known." The knowledge of God is our key to overcoming the false ideas of the old man. (Ephesians 1:17; Colossians 3:10; James 3:13; II Peter 1:3, 3:18) When we turn from the lies and misrepresentations of the world and start listening to God's truth, we are able to repair the old mentality. (Romans 12:2, II Corinthians 10:4) A recent cartoon showed God speaking to Adam and Eve as they stood in front of the Tree of the Knowledge of Good and Evil. His message was, "Eat all the apples you like, but stay away from the Tree of Idiocy." His finger was pointing to a tree filled with television screens and computer monitors. Even though the comic strip "pushes the envelope," it does communicate a real truth. Many years before computers became household items and the Internet was even birthed, Dr. Lester Sumrall had a vision in which the devil appeared to him and said that he had a plan to destroy the minds of America. The next thing that Dr. Sumrall saw in that revelation was the image of a television screen (of course, we later understood that it could also have been a computer monitor). Satan is using the arenas of media, entertainment, and sports to take over the minds of our generation; however, believers can and must rise up and take responsible places of authority in these areas of interface to proclaim God's truth and present godly and moral role models.

Next, came the valley gate. (verse 3:13) This gate overlooked the Kidron Valley – a massive cemetery filled with monuments to remind the people of their past kings and other significant elements of their history. Since such memorials symbolize "teaching moments," opportunities to teach a new generation about the truths a former generation had learned (Joshua 4:6, 21), this gate must represent education. Today, the gate of education has been taken over by those who represent anything but the truth that has been passed down from our fathers. The homosexual agenda, Islamic culture and theology, evolution, and humanism fill our textbooks, while even the slightest mention of God – a quote from the Bible, a list of the Ten Commandments, or prayer in Jesus' name – can end in a legal suit and suspension of students and termination of teachers. Christians must aggressively retake this gate and turn it back into an interface for God rather than a portal for the devil's lies.

In spite of its repulsive name, the dung gate is a very important interface. (verse 3:14) It was from this gate that the residents of the city hauled their refuse to be burned in the Valley of Hinnom; therefore, this gate represents infrastructure. The public works system implemented here speaks of a society that works together for the common good. However, simple sanitation, working utilities, safe roads, and other civil services are lacking in most countries. When these basic elements of infrastructure are lacking, people suffer tremendously. The lack of proper sanitation results in tremendous suffering and death from such diseases as malaria, cholera, and dysentery – all of which are easily prevented, yet difficult to treat. Many times, it is Christian missionaries who make the first breakthroughs in these areas. Their work breaks the bondage of poverty, disease, and death. Until simple infrastructure is in place, advancement is impossible. William Carey, the father of modern missions, took five months by steamer to get to Calcutta, but today's advanced technology and the infrastructure of modern airports in India make it possible for a missionary to reach the same destination within one day. If you can't get there, you can't minister; but if you can get there, you can do a world of good. I have personally known of several occasions when the missionaries and local pastors in mission areas have sent messages back to mission groups in America asking them to stop sending food, medicine, and literature because there simply was no way to store, transport, or distribute the aid. The devil had established gates of hell in these countries through the infrastructure – or actually the lack thereof – and was, therefore, able to keep the people poor, sick, and lost.

The water gate (verse 3:26) marked the entrance of Hezekiah's Tunnel that brought fresh water into the city from outside the wall. This tunnel was an engineering breakthrough that allowed the people inside to weather extended assaults and blockades from invading armies. I see this gate as representing enterprise and ingenuity. Many countries and masses of individuals are held in poverty because of the lack of enterprise and ingenuity. Africa is the poorest continent on earth, but it is also the richest in natural resources, including uranium, titanium, manganese, potash, cobalt, platinum, oil, gas, gold, and diamonds. I discovered that many people in Hungary are hungry, even though they have enough land to raise their own food. The simple problem is that they don't see the potential of turning their little plots of ground into subsistence farms. I learned that this problem is especially bad among the gypsy population – even after they are born again. Because Satan has turned ingenuity and enterprise into a gate of hell, these believers fall back into the old lifestyle of cheating, stealing, and illegal activity to feed themselves and their families. People around the world are held in the slavery of poverty because they lack the insight into how to claim God's free gifts. But godly men and women can take hold of the gate of enterprise and ingenuity through God-given creativity and divine inspiration and turn these strongholds of poverty into interfaces of God's supernatural prosperity. Let me share just one simple example of how easy it can be. My uncle, who worked for a sheet metal company, noticed that every day the company was throwing away a number of the large sheers used to cut the metal because the handles were broken. When he asked the owner of the company if he could have the broken tools, the gentleman gladly gave them to him but asked why he wanted the broken implements. My uncle answered that only one handle was broken on each tool. His plan was to take the good handle of each set of sheers and put a right-hand handle together with a left-hand handle to make a new working instrument. The lack of ingenuity was costing the company hundreds of dollars each month.

Nehemiah's eighth gate was the horse gate (verse 3:28), so called because it led to the stables where the nation's warhorses were housed. This gate represents military and government. Governments and military powers have effectively crushed evangelism and stopped open ministry in many parts of the world. I remember the time when a pastor in one restricted country got up in the middle of my sermon and began closing all the curtains because he sensed that we were being watched, even though we had a permit to hold the Christian meeting – a permit which, by the way, was only granted at the last minute in what seemed like the government's attempt to keep us from being able to gather a full congregation, even though we technically had the constitutional right to meet. This same pastor was always careful to never meet me in public because he knew that being seen with a Westerner was all that was needed to precipitate a government sanction. And it did happen that, shortly after my visit, his house was searched in an attempt to find illegal Christian "contraband." But the truth is that we don't have to let the devil turn governments and armies into his strongholds. Just like the Iron Curtain came down, country after country has

26

surrendered to the prayers and faith of God's people. In Acts 12:10, we read the story of how the army arrested Peter but God opened the iron gate for him to walk out a free man. We, too, can prove that no government or army is more powerful than the name of the Lord our God. (Psalm 20:7)

Next to the horse gate was the east gate. (verse 3:29) This gate was considered the avenue through which the messiah would enter the city. With this in mind, we can assume that its very presence inspired patriotism and hope; therefore, I see it as representing national spirit. While all other nations count their wealth by the financial GNP (Gross National Product) index, the country of Bhutan uses an emotional indicator – the GNH (Gross National Happiness) index. Such an indicator shows the significance of the emotional or "spirit" factor. History is full of examples of little nations that conquered much larger nations against impossible odds – David and Goliath, for example – simply because of the emotional element of "national spirit." The spirit of jihad is a prime example of the demonic use of this factor. Israeli Prime Minister Benjamin Netanyahu addressed the UN a few days after Iran's president made a scathing speech to the same body. The Jewish leader's speech was intended to reiterate that the most dangerous country on the planet must not be allowed to arm itself with nuclear weapons, especially in light of Iran's recent threat to make a pre-emptive strike against the Jewish state. Showing a diagram of a bomb, the Israeli Prime Minister pointed out that Iran was nearing the ninety-percent mark on their uranium enrichment project and moving into the final stage of their armament program. He warned that the world had until the following spring, or the next summer at the most, before the bomb would be ready. Prime Minister Netanyahu then pointed out that deterrence would not work with Iran as it did with the Soviets because the Soviets chose existence over ideology and stated, "The militant jihadists behave very differently from secular Marxists. There were no Soviet suicide bombers. Yet, Iran produces hordes of them." Call it patriotism, national spirit, or jihad – this emotional factor can be more prominent than government and military. All we need to do is look at the coups from within the populace that have changed the course of history – the American Revolution, the French Revolution, Tiananmen Square, the Arab Spring, and the list goes on to include smaller resistance movements such as ones I've personally witnessed in Nepal and Burma. It's time that believers begin to influence our national spirit and turn the spirits of the people into a groundswell of grassroots revival. (II Chronicles 7:14)

The last gate that Nehemiah repaired was the gate Miphkad. (verse 3:31) The name of this gate is translated in various ways including, "inspection," "judgment," and "census." If we follow the last translation, it becomes clear that the gate signifies the numbering of the people, which addresses directly the significance of family; therefore, I opt to view this gate as representing the significance of family in society. A census is not simply a headcount; rather, it is an analysis of how many people fall into various categories such as socio-economic and ethnic divisions. The book of Numbers is an excellent display of how the entire population census of Israel was categorized by tribes, clans, and families. To emphasize the importance of family in society, let me present one startling fact: we actually use the number of fatherless homes in an area to determine the number and size of jails to build in that jurisdiction! The simple act of gathering the family around the dinner table makes a significant difference in the overall wellbeing of society. Children from families that practice regular meals together are much less likely to be overweight, are six times less likely to smoke marijuana, are two thirds less likely to use laxatives, diet pills, and purging to control weight, and have lower rates of smoking, alcohol use, and depression. Plus they almost invariably earn better grades. Christians can, and must, take back the gate of family and turn it into an interface for heaven rather than an open door for Satan.

It is in the home that we learn the restraints that keep us from falling into the traps that the enemy has set to ensnare us. For example, immorality is specifically defined as a path (gate)

28

that leads directly to hell. (Proverbs 7:27) Jesus told us that the gate that goes to destruction is wide, meaning that it has nor restrictions, barriers, or hindrances. (Matthew 7:13-14) Where else than in the home do we find the instruction that helps deter us from those seeming easy paths to destruction (hell)?

Two more gates are mentioned in the book of Nehemiah. Even though it is not mentioned that these were specifically on Nehemiah's list of repairs, it is unthinkable that he would have left them vulnerable. The first is the gate of Ephraim. (verse 8:16) Ephraim's name means "fruitfulness," signifying the abundant material and financial blessings of God. Hence, I see this gate as referring to finance. First Timothy 6:10 tells us that the love of money is the root of all evil, and it only takes a simple look around us to see how greed in the financial world has fostered all sorts of evil, including child labor, sweat shops, slave labor, human trafficking, labor camps in Africa where women and children use mercury to extract metal with their bare hands, precious metal reclamation processes in India where the workers breathe harmful fumes while melting down old computers and cell phones, and the list of such atrocities seems endless. It is time that godly men and women step into the world of finance to stop such injustices. As Tunde Bakare, a prominent African church leader says, "God is ready to raise up a new breed without greed!"

Nehemiah's final gate was the prison gate (verse 12:39), which obviously speaks of law enforcement and justice systems. The fact that this gate was in close proximity to the local jail speaks to us of the significance of penal and correctional institutions and practices in any society. Without a godly influence in our courts and prisons, guilty men who can afford powerful lawyers walk the streets while innocent men and petty criminals are sent to facilities that are essentially crime colleges where they are educated in advanced lessons of evil so that society suffers even more when they are released. Instead, we should make our criminal justice system a major area for evangelism where men and women can find a way out of the real prison they are living in – the bondage of sin.

Remember that Deuteronomy 16:18-20 specifically mentions that judges are to be seated at the city gates – gates that should be the entrance of heaven, not the stronghold of hell.

We are directed to attack the gates of our enemies and take possession.

> *That in blessing I will bless thee [Abraham],*
> *and in multiplying I will multiply thy seed as*
> *the stars of the heaven, and as the sand*
> *which is upon the sea shore; and thy seed*
> *shall possess the gate of his enemies.*
> (Genesis 22:17)
> *And they blessed Rebekah, and said unto her,*
> *Thou art our sister, be thou the mother of*
> *thousands of millions, and let thy seed*
> *possess the gate of those which hate them.*
> (Genesis 24:60)

The church is called to fill all – all the gates of society – so that we can determine culture. (Ephesians 4:10) To illustrate the reality of our ability to actually turn the gates of hell into gates of heaven, I'd like to share just two stories of how demonic strongholds were transformed into entranceways into heaven. The first story will come from the Bible and the second from contemporary history.

In Mark chapter five, we read the thrilling story of how Jesus cast the legion of demons out of a man who was fully possessed by the devil. Before Jesus arrived, the demoniac broke all the ropes the people used to try to restrain him, ran naked in the graveyards, and cut himself with stones. But when Jesus showed up, the wild man was set free and the demons ran into the sea and drowned themselves. Even though the people of the region were amazed to see this wild man now clothed and in his right mind, they demanded that Jesus leave town immediately. The young man's final request as Jesus departed was that he be allowed to go with Him. Jesus refused and insisted that the man return to his family and friends and tell them of the great things that had happened to him. (verse 19) The next verse confirms that he did exactly that and tells us specifically that the place he went to was Decapolis. The next time we see mention of Decapolis is in Mark 7:31 when Jesus returned to the area. This time, He was received readily and even drew a crowd of over four thousand to listen to His message. (verse 8:9) What made the difference between the time He was run out of town and the time He was accepted with open arms? My guess is that it was the testimony of the freed demoniac. His witness had turned the stronghold of Satan into a gateway to heaven.

My second story comes from the life of Dr. Lester Sumrall, one of the great authorities on dealing with demonic power. When the Lord spoke to him to go to the Philippines to raise up a ministry there, He promised, "I will do more for you there than I have done for you anywhere else in your ministry." Knowing that there had never been any major Protestant revival in the Philippines in the history of the country and that there were very few Christians in the city, Bro. Sumrall went to Manila with great anticipation of what God was going to do. For the first several months, there were only a handful of people in his church. About the time the congregation had grown to fifty people, the Lord began impressing him that he was to build a barn to hold the coming harvest. So, he started building a church that would seat twenty-five hundred people. He reasoned that he needed a building of at least that size since he had left a church in the US with over a thousand adults and a thousand children in Sunday school each week, and the Lord had promised something bigger in the Philippines. Everybody begged him not to do it. His denomination thought he would make them the laughingstock of the entire world – building a church to seat over two thousand when he only had fifty members. Protestant missionaries and prominent church leaders came to Manila to stop him because they were afraid he would take their members to fill his church. But he refused to be swayed by their arguments because he knew that God would bring a revival such as the Philippines had never seen.

One night while he was getting ready for bed, Bro. Sumrall and his wife listened to the evening news. Suddenly, bloodcurdling screaming and horrifying howls come across the airwaves. The news feature was the story of a young girl incarcerated in the Bilibid Prison in Manila who had been mysteriously bitten by unseen teeth. Medical doctors and prison wardens observed as tooth marks and blood mysteriously appeared on her body. From his previous missionary work, Bro. Sumrall recognized that this was demon power tormenting her; so, he got out of bed and lay on the floor praying and travailing, asking God to send somebody to deliver her from the demon power. But the Lord answered him, "If you don't do it, it won't happen. You are the only one in this city who knows how to cast the devil out of her." At that point, Bro. Sumrall had no way of knowing that this was the key that would unlock the gate of hell in the Philippines.

He spent that night in prayer and fasting. The next morning, he called the contractor who was building the church. Since he was a personal friend of the mayor, the contractor got Bro. Sumrall an appointment to see the mayor of the city who granted permission for Bro. Sumrall to go into Bilibid Prison and pray for the girl. The story of the girl had already hit the international news, and the city had sent out appeals for church leaders, psychiatrists, or somebody to come and help her – but no one was able to deliver her. Bro. Sumrall went to pray for her, but he did not get a total victory the first day; so he went back again the second and third days. After three days of fasting and prayer, he spoke to the spirit, and it left. Not only was the girl set free, a remarkable thing happened in the city. Unbeknownst to Bro. Sumrall, the demon spirit that was controlling that young girl was the principality spirit that ruled the entire Philippines. And as soon as his power was broken, the entire spirit realm of the Philippines became defenseless against the attack of the gospel.

When Bro. Sumrall was ushered back into the mayor's office with the good news that the girl had been freed, the mayor was so pleased that he asked what Bro. Sumrall wanted in return. His request was for permission to have large open-air revival meetings every night on the main plaza of the city. Within a six-week period, one hundred fifty thousand people were converted to Christ. When construction of the church was complete and the dedication service was held, the church was so jammed that a large mass of people could not get inside.

How can we make this same kind of impact when we determine to attack the gates of hell in our society? I believe that there are three simple steps: pray, act, be.

Paul gave us a concise and clear mandate to pray:

> *I exhort therefore, that, first of all, supplications, prayers, intercessions, and giving of thanks, be made for all men; For kings, and for all that are in authority; that we may lead a quiet and peaceable life in all godliness and honesty. For this is good and acceptable in the sight of God our Saviour.* (I Timothy 2:1-3)

The life of Queen Esther gives us a stunning example of how we can step up to the plate and take aggressive action:

> *Then Mordecai commanded to answer Esther, Think not with thyself that thou shalt escape in the king's house, more than all the Jews. For if thou altogether holdest thy peace at this time, then shall there enlargement and deliverance arise to the Jews from another place; but thou and thy father's house shall be destroyed: and who knoweth whether thou art come to the kingdom for such a time as this? Then Esther bade them return Mordecai this answer, Go, gather together all the Jews that are present in Shushan, and fast ye for me, and neither eat nor drink three days, night or*

day: I also and my maidens will fast likewise; and so will I go in unto the king, which is not according to the law: and if I perish, I perish. (Esther 4:13-16)

Even though the verse I am going to offer next is generally used to refer to prayer and intercession, its context does not suggest that interpretation at all. Rather, its clear message is that we need to actually physically step into the places where God's presence is not being felt and be God's man or woman literally standing there, making His presence known. If this means that we need to run for office, then we must do so. If it means that we be educated in order to qualify for a position, then we must do so. If it means that we must change careers to be at the place God wants us, then we must do so. Whatever it takes is what we must do!

And I sought for a man among them, that should make up the hedge, and stand in the gap before me for the land, that I should not destroy it: but I found none. (Ezekiel 22:30)

God never sends us to a door, window, or gate unless He makes sure that we have the necessary key or keys to get through those interfaces. In the passage in Revelation 3:7 that promises us an open door to the world, the key that opened that interface is described as David's key. Even though Matthew 16:19 does not specifically mention windows, Jesus declared in that verse that He was passing along the keys to heaven to us. In Revelation 1:18, Jesus blatantly affirmed that He was holding the keys of hell. Although He doesn't actually mention that those keys fit into the lock on hell's gates, it isn't a major leap of logic to make that assumption.

When I think of the key of David mentioned in the letter to the church at Philadelphia, I immediately realize that it is unlike any key that I have ever seen because it opens doors that can never be shut and closes doors so that no one will ever be able to open them. I can remember picking many locks to get into cars that had been locked with the keys inside. I can easily recall the trip from South Korea when our entire group had their suitcase locks picked or broken open. I also remember failing to get into doors, even though I had the keys that unlocked the main lock, because there was a safety or dead bolt on the door.

The reference to the key of David, is apparently drawn from Isaiah 22:22, *And the key of the house of David will I lay upon his shoulder; so he shall open, and none shall shut; and he shall shut, and none shall open.* In this verse, the prophet is making reference to Eliakim, the son of Hilkiah, as the one who will receive this supernatural key. This biblical character's historic role is recounted twice – in II Kings chapters eighteen and nineteen and again in Isaiah chapters thirty-six and thirty-seven. In both records, the specific reason given for the deliverance of the city was that it was for the sake of David. (II Kings 19:34 and Isaiah 37:35) In some way, Eliakim stood in the stead of David and held his key. Eliakim's significant contribution was the stance he took against the Assyrian messenger who tried to intimidate the people of Jerusalem into surrendering to his army. Eliakim stood up to him with faith and confidence in God until the Lord caused the invading army to miraculously retreat.

Though the scriptures do not specifically identify what this key was, it is easy for us to look into the life of David and find one characteristic that seems to stand out that could have made the difference between him and any others who lacked this quality. It is likely that we need not go any further than the criteria set for his selection for the throne of Israel. After Samuel had surveyed the seven older sons of Jesse without finding a worthy candidate, the Lord revealed to him that he was looking at the wrong score card when evaluating his options. God made His point that the heart of the matter is actually the matter of the heart.

But the LORD said unto Samuel, Look not on his countenance, or on the height of his stature; because I have refused him: for the LORD seeth not as man seeth; for man looketh on the outward appearance, but the LORD looketh on the heart. (I Samuel 16:7)

David obviously understood that this was his key to success and determined to keep his heart in a perfect relationship with his God. *I will behave myself wisely in a perfect way. O when wilt thou come unto me? I will walk within my house with a perfect heart.* (Psalm 101:2) Even after he sinned with Bathsheba and had her husband killed, the king's prayer was that God would re-establish his heart before Him. (Psalm 51:10) Consequently, the New Testament characterizes David as being a man after God's own heart. (Acts 13:22) He desired to pass this spiritual key on to his son Solomon who was to succeed him on the throne. First Chronicles 28:9 records David's instructions to Solomon that he should serve the Lord with a perfect heart. In verse nineteen of the following chapter, we find David in prayer for his son, interceding that the Lord would give him a perfect heart. Unfortunately, the biblical summation of Solomon's life is that *his heart was not perfect with the LORD his God, as was the heart of David his father.* (I Kings 11:4)

In the testimony of one of the subsequent kings, II Chronicles 25:2 records that Amaziah did that which was right in the sight of the Lord, yet not with a perfect heart. He was passionate in his campaign to stamp out idolatry; yet, he failed to passionately pursue the Lord Himself. Asa before him received what is likely the greatest promise in the scripture: *The eyes of the LORD run to and fro throughout the whole earth, to shew himself strong in the behalf of them whose heart is perfect toward him.* (II Chronicles 16:9) This is the universal blessing and promise of intervention by God that can only be unlocked with the key of David – a perfect heart before the Lord. It was the promise extended to the church at Philadelphia.

When Jesus told the parable of the dividing of the sheep and goats in Matthew 25:31-46, He emphasized that our response to the hurting and hungry of the world is the yardstick by which He measures those who claim to be believers. In the parable of Lazarus and the rich man (Luke 16:19-25), He further illustrated the tragedy of lacking the heart to help the poor. There is a lesson about heart attitudes to be learned from these parables. When David had to "face the music" concerning committing adultery with Bathsheba and having her husband killed, his repentance prayer was that he had sinned against God and God alone. (Psalm 51:4) David had violated a virtuous woman and killed an innocent man; yet, he saw only God as his victim. The point that Jesus made in the parable is that when we do evil or good to even the least human, we have actually acted either for or against Him. The same lesson is expressed in the encounter between Jesus and Saul of Tarsus on the road to Damascus when the Lord introduced Himself as *Jesus whom thou persecutest*. (Acts 9:5) Saul's hostilities had been against humans, but Jesus "took them personally." What seems to be the point? The final analysis of the matter seems to be that, in order to have the perfect heart as our key to open the doors before us, we must have a heart that is continually seeing our each and every action as if it were for or against God Himself. In recent years, much has been said and written about living life by the motto, "WWJD – What Would Jesus Do?" A more biblical maxim for life might be "WWIDFJ – What Would I Do For Jesus?" Just doing what Jesus would do might land us in the same spot as some of the people described in I Corinthians chapter thirteen – those who gave their food to feed the poor and even gave their bodies to be burned as martyrs. Unfortunately, even these noblest of deeds didn't count for anything in God's sight because they were done out of the wrong motive. However, if we fall so desperately in love with Jesus that we see Him in every situation and in every human condition, we will hear the Master's approving words, *Come, ye blessed of my Father, inherit the kingdom prepared for you from the foundation of the world.* (Matthew 25:34)

There is one other unique quality that we need to notice about the church at Philadelphia: of all seven churches, they are the only ones indicated as having any relationship to the Word of God. Not only that, they are twice commended for their faithfulness to God's Word. (verses 3:8, 10) Though all seven churches are admonished to hear what the Spirit is saying, apparently only this one listened and heeded. Like David, they recognized that the key to having a perfect heart was to hide God's Word in their hearts. (Psalm 119:11) A heart renewed through interfacing with the Word of God will make us a success at every other interface we meet.

Jesus described the keys that open the windows of heaven in Matthew 16:19, *And I will give unto thee the keys of the kingdom of heaven: and whatsoever thou shalt bind on earth shall be bound in heaven: and whatsoever thou shalt loose on earth shall be loosed in heaven.* Before we jump to any conclusions as to what He was intending to say here, let's take a minute to look at some more modern translations of this passage:

> *I will give you the keys of the Kingdom of the Heavens; and whatever you bind on earth shall remain bound in Heaven, and whatever you loose on earth shall remain loosed in Heaven.* (Weymouth's New Testament)
> *And I will give the keys of the kingdom of Heaven to you. And whatever you may bind on earth shall occur, having been bound in Heaven, and whatever you may loose on earth shall occur, having been loosed in Heaven.* (Modern King James Version)
> *And I will give to thee the keys of the reign of the heavens, and whatever thou mayest bind upon the earth shall be having been bound in the heavens, and whatever thou mayest loose upon the earth shall be having been loosed in the heavens.* (Young's Literal Translation)

Notice that the wording in each of these renditions of the passage suggests that what happens in heaven is not the result of what is done on earth; rather, it is actually a pre-existing condition. Weymouth's Translation uses the word "remain," implying that the determination is already made and that our use of the key to heaven's window is essentially a spoken affirmation in agreement with what is already predetermined. The Modern King James and Young's Literal Translation both use the wording "having been," which again reflects the idea that the outcome is already determined prior to the prayers or proclamations of believers. All these translations are making an attempt to convey the actual message of the Greek text, which implies that the key Jesus was giving us was not so much the ability to self-determine destinies and outcomes. Rather it is the ability to know the mind of God well enough that we are actually speaking out His mind on the matter whenever we pray or proclaim anything. (I Corinthians 2:16) To get a clear vision of what Jesus was trying to tell us, let's look at a very familiar – yet often misunderstood – passage on intercession:

> *And take the helmet of salvation, and the sword of the Spirit, which is the word of God: Praying always with all prayer and supplication in the Spirit, and watching thereunto with all perseverance and supplication for all saints.* (Ephesians 6:17-18)

In these verses, Paul seems to be making an intentional connection between prayer and the Word of God in that he lists both of them as being connected with the Spirit. The Word of God is defined as the sword of the Spirit, and prayer is specified as being in the Spirit. Remembering a few other biblical truths, we can begin to see the message behind this connection. According to Psalm 119:89, God's Word is forever settled in heaven. Even though His ways are much higher than our ways (Isaiah 55:9) and His judgments beyond finding out (Romans 11:33), He has made a way, through the work of the Holy Spirit, for us to know all the benefits He has prepared for us (I Corinthians 2:9-10, John 14:26). When the Holy Spirit reveals to us the specific promises from the Word of God that we need to use as the sword of the Spirit when He is directing our prayers, then we develop a confidence in our prayers (I John 5:14-15) and an assurance that everything is going to work out just right (Romans 8:26-28). God already has our success determined in heaven, but we must use a special key to open the windows so that those heavenly blessings can be released upon us. That key is the ability to pray under the direction of the Holy Spirit so that our prayers are not off base, but in total alignment with what God has already bound and loosed in heaven. Perhaps this is what Jesus meant when He said that the Jewish leaders had taken away the key of knowledge and refused to enter into the kingdom of God themselves and had also blocked others from entering in. (Luke 11:52) They had turned revelation into religion and were no longer hearing from the Spirit of God. Certainly, this is why Jesus' prayer that God's will be done on earth as it is in heaven was made a major point in His model prayer. (Matthew 6:10, Luke 11:2)

When Jesus proclaimed that He was holding the key to hell, He specifically said that the reason He was in possession of this key was because He had been dead but was now alive, *I am he that liveth, and was dead; and, behold, I am alive for evermore, Amen; and have the keys of hell and of death.* (Revelation 1:18) By going into the very throne room of the kingdom of darkness through death, Jesus was able to retrieve the keys that unlock the gates of death and hell. And as He exited from Satan's dark domain on Resurrection morn, He left those gateways vulnerable and defenseless – vulnerable and defenseless because He intended to deliver the keys of those demonic strongholds to His bride, the church. But we must go through the same process as Jesus did to qualify to use those keys – we must die and be resurrected to new life. In our case, the death and resurrection we are to experience is a spiritual reality, not the physical cross, tomb, and Sheol of the first Easter.

Therefore we are buried with him by baptism into death: that like as Christ was raised up from the dead by the glory of the Father, even so we also should walk in newness of life. (Romans 6:4)

Knowing this, that our old man is crucified with him, that the body of sin might be destroyed, that henceforth we should not serve sin. (Romans 6:6)

Likewise reckon ye also yourselves to be dead indeed unto sin, but alive unto God through Jesus Christ our Lord. (Romans 6:11)

For if ye live after the flesh, ye shall die: but if ye through the Spirit do mortify the deeds of the body, ye shall live. (Romans 8:13)

But put ye on the Lord Jesus Christ, and make not provision for the flesh, to fulfil the lusts thereof. (Romans 13:14)

I am crucified with Christ: nevertheless I live; yet not I, but Christ liveth in me: and the life which I now live in the flesh I live by the faith of the Son of God, who loved me, and gave himself for me. (Galatians 2:20)

And you hath he quickened, who were dead in trespasses and sins. (Ephesians 2:1)

That ye put off concerning the former conversation the old man, which is corrupt according to the deceitful lusts. (Ephesians 4:22)

Buried with him in baptism, wherein also ye are risen with him through the faith of the operation of God, who hath raised him from the dead. And you, being dead in your sins and the uncircumcision of your flesh, hath he quickened together with him, having forgiven you all trespasses. (Colossians 2:12-13)

Mortify therefore your members which are upon the earth; fornication, uncleanness, inordinate affection, evil concupiscence, and covetousness, which is idolatry. (Colossians 3:5)

Lie not one to another, seeing that ye have put off the old man with his deeds. (Colossians 3:9)

Forasmuch then as Christ hath suffered for us in the flesh, arm yourselves likewise with the same mind: for he that hath suffered in the flesh hath ceased from sin; That he no longer should live the rest of his time in the flesh to the lusts of men, but to the will of God. (I Peter 4:1-2)

It is only through such a death to the old sinful nature and a resurrection to the life of Christ within us that we have the power and authority to attack and take control of the gates of hell. Many people are afraid to take a place of power and influence in politics or any position in society because they believe that power and money will corrupt them. The truth is that position and money cannot corrupt honest men; all that power and money can do is expose the corruption that is already lying beneath the surface in sinful men who have been masquerading as honest ones.

When John wrote to the young men in his first epistle, he said something very interesting. He told them, "You are the young men. You are the conquerors. I write to you because you have overcome the wicked one." (I John 2:13-14) But then he goes on to say something that almost startles us, *Love not the world, neither the things of the world.* (verse 15) It amazes me that we can be overcomers and conquerors, yet still love the enemy. We can be the ones who have overcome the wicked one and have defeated the devil, but still have a love in our hearts for the things that belong to the enemy's camp. Joshua faced this same problem when he went in to possess the gates of the enemy. (Joshua chapter seven) When he marched around the city of Jericho and the walls came tumbling down, one of his men named Achan went into the enemy's camp and loved the things he saw inside the city. Achan's mind raced as he made his reconnaissance mission into the city to determine how to destroy it, "I must have some of this gold and some of these Babylonian garments." He still loved the things of Jericho, even though he had marched around its walls thirteen times and he had screamed at the top of his voice to see the walls come tumbling down. He overcame the city of Jericho, but he still loved the things of Jericho; therefore, he took them and hid them in his tent. A few days later, the armies of Joshua were defeated at the battle of Ai – all because of this man who, even though he was an overcomer, still loved the things in the enemy's camp.

We also know the story of King Saul who had the same problem because he went off and conquered the Amalakites but brought back some of the prize sheep and cattle and kept the king alive. (I Samuel chapter fifteen) His alibi to the prophet was that he had saved them for a sacrifice, and maybe he had – we don't know. But still there was something inside him that loved those things of the enemy even though he had conquered the enemy. Even though he had overcome the external enemy, he had not overcome the enemy within himself! There was still love in his heart for the enemy and the things of the enemy.

We can overcome the wicked one, but we can still love the world and the things that are in it. John goes on to tell us that the things that are in the world are the lust of the flesh, the lust of the eyes, and the pride of life. (I John 2:16)

We usually associate the lust of the flesh with sexual sin. The lust of the eyes has to do with the things that we can look at, that we can have, that we can possess – the things that make your eyes bulge out when you go to the shopping mall. The pride of life has to do with our promotions, our desire to be somebody, and our need to have a title. The lust of the flesh (sexual sin); the lust of the eyes (our salary and the things that it can get); the pride of life (our status and the position that it can buy). We must not love the "S"s: sex, salary, and status.

We can still make the mistake of loving those things even though we are conquerors, even though we are overcomers.

Dr. Lester Sumrall always said that there are three things that capture ministers: the gold, the gals, and the glory. What are those? The "gold" is our salary, the lust of the eyes. The "gals" is sexual sin, the lust of the flesh. The "glory" is our status, the pride of life. It is not enough to be an overcomer of the wicked one; we also have to be those people who are overcomers of our own human nature that still loves the world and the things that are in it.

It is interesting to me how John shifts from "love" to "lust." Notice that he said that we <u>love</u> the world and the things of the world; then he immediately described the things in the world, calling them the <u>lust</u> of the eyes and the <u>lust</u> of the flesh. We try to think of lust and love as two separate entities. When it comes to anything other than the undiluted love of God, our love or our attachment will immediately turn to lust. We have to be so very careful.

Unless we are truly dead to sin and the lust thereof and alive to Christ and Christ alone, we run a very dangerous risk of not only failing to be able to take the gates of hell but of actually being ensnared by them. But Jesus told us that those gates would not be able to prevail against our aggressive attack. Why? Because He gave us the key of becoming new creatures in Him.

> *Therefore if any man be in Christ, he is a new creature: old things are passed away; behold, all things are become new.* (II Corinthians 5:17)
> *For he hath made him to be sin for us, who knew no sin; that we might be made the righteousness of God in him.* (II Corinthians 5:21)
> *According as he hath chosen us in him before the foundation of the world, that we should*

be holy and without blame before him in love. (Ephesians 1:4)
And be found in him, not having mine own righteousness, which is of the law, but that which is through the faith of Christ, the righteousness which is of God by faith. (Philippians 3:9)

I'd like to close this discussion with the dynamic apostolic prayer that Paul prayed over the Ephesian church when he was trying to encourage them to understand these same truths. Although he didn't refer to these truths specifically as keys to the doors of the world around us, the windows of heaven, and the gates of hell, he made powerful intercession, invoking each principle as part of the full key ring of a godly heart of love, the revelation of the Holy Spirit, and the new life through association with the death and resurrection of Christ.

[I] *Cease not to give thanks for you, making mention of you in my prayers; That the God of our Lord Jesus Christ, the Father of glory, may give unto you the spirit of wisdom and revelation in the knowledge of him: The eyes of your understanding being enlightened; that ye may know what is the hope of his calling, and what the riches of the glory of his inheritance in the saints, And what is the exceeding greatness of his power to us-ward who believe, according to the working of his mighty power, Which he wrought in Christ, when he raised him from the dead, and set him at his own right hand in the heavenly places, Far above all principality, and power, and might, and dominion, and every name that is named, not only in this world, but also in that which is to come: And hath put all things under his feet, and gave him to be the head over all things to the church,*

Which is his body, the fulness of him that filleth all in all...For this cause I bow my knees unto the Father of our Lord Jesus Christ, Of whom the whole family in heaven and earth is named, That he would grant you, according to the riches of his glory, to be strengthened with might by his Spirit in the inner man; That Christ may dwell in your hearts by faith; that ye, being rooted and grounded in love, May be able to comprehend with all saints what is the breadth, and length, and depth, and height; And to know the love of Christ, which passeth knowledge, that ye might be filled with all the fulness of God. Now unto him that is able to do exceeding abundantly above all that we ask or think, according to the power that worketh in us, Unto him be glory in the church by Christ Jesus throughout all ages, world without end. Amen. (Ephesians 1:16-23, 3:14-21)

Chapter Two
Awake

When the little boy's mom put her finger to her lips and blew out a little "shh" to remind him to be quiet in church, the lad looked quizzically back at his mother and whispered, "How come do we have to be quiet in church? Are there people trying to sleep?" Yes, worshipers – including myself – do occasionally nod off during Sunday service. In fact, one pastor brags that he is a more effective preacher than the Apostle Paul since it is recorded that Paul only had one person (Acts 20:9) to doze off during the entire history of his ministry, while he could often put half the congregation to sleep with only one sermon. If we consider the spiritual drowsiness in the church, the percentage is probably even much higher than this preacher's rating with people falling physically asleep. Therefore, it is no wonder that the Spirit rings out a great wake-up call to the Body of Christ, *Awake thou that sleepest, and arise from the dead, and Christ shall give thee light.* (Ephesians 5:14) But before we address His call that shakes us out of our slumber, it would be good to look at exactly what sleep is anyway.

In the physical realm, a good night of sleep is an absolute necessity. Along with nutrition, sleep actually fuels our lives because our bodies turn their energy inward when we sleep. Instead of expending energy on physical activities as our bodies do while we are awake, our sleeping bodies focus on repairing damaged cells and tissues and recharging the immune system by building up a new contingent of natural killer cells. During sleep, our growth hormones are actively repairing damaged tissue in adults and building new tissue in children. Additionally, our bodies take time to undo the corrosive effects of the stress that we have encountered during the day. Even short snoozes can have regenerative qualities. A study done in Greece showed an inverse relationship between napping and heart attacks. Work-related studies have proven that a twenty-six-minute nap can boost job performance by more than one third, and such mid-day dozes will not hinder our nighttime rest. Studies indicate that even an hour-and-a-half nap in the early afternoon will not affect our night's sleep.

Although we should keep sleep at the top of our priorities list each day, seventy-one percent of adults and eighty-five percent of teens don't get the recommended amount of sleep. With such high percentages, it is actually surprising that only twenty-eight percent of teens report falling asleep in school and more people don't get fired for sleeping on the job. In the same way that making conscious choices about the food we eat helps put us on the path to optimal health, getting sound sleep each night can go a long way toward promoting our best quality of life. Just as we all need air, water, and food to survive, we also need sleep to be healthy. We would probably be amazed at the positive impact that making optimal sleep a priority in our lives would have on both our mental and physical well-being. Unfortunately, too many of us sacrifice good sleep in order to gain more time for our work or other activities – a direct contradiction to scriptural principles:

> *Except the LORD build the house, they labour in vain that build it: except the LORD keep the city, the watchman waketh but in vain. It is vain for you to rise up early, to sit up late, to eat the bread of sorrows: for so he giveth his beloved sleep.* (Psalm 127:2)

Three indicators signify good quality sleep: the ability to fall asleep within five minutes of lying down, the tendency to sleep through the night without waking, and the capability of rising the next morning feeling rested and refreshed. If these indicators are not confirming that we are getting the proper sleep, we need to examine the variables in our lives to see what needs to be altered. Obviously, finding the right bed is one of the major factors to sleeping "tight" – a figure of speech that harkens to Shakespeare's time when mattresses were secured on bed frames by ropes that were pulled on to make the bed firmer. However, the most significant changes needed are not in our environment but in our lifestyles. To find the real culprits in sleep loss, we usually need to look no further than our own daily routines and habits to see where we are overtaxing ourselves. It has been said that a good night's sleep actually starts the second we wake up in the morning because all the activities of the day figure into our ability to sleep well at night. For example, exercise helps set the biological clock to a consistent sleep-wake pattern; therefore, lack of proper physical activity can cause sleep problems. Diet can also help regulate our sleep patterns. Obviously, we need to avoid sugar and caffeine for a period of time prior to retiring for the evening. Eating a high-carb meal, such as rice, four hours before bed can cut in half the time it takes to fall asleep. Another factor that plays significantly into our ability to sleep well is the transition of winding down our daily activity. Research indicates that most of us spend the final hour of our day doing household chores, taking care of children, or catching up on work – all activities that stimulate rather than settle us down. Interestingly enough, the most powerful sleep inducer is sexual intercourse; therefore, a good marital relationship should also promote good sleep patterns and habits. In addition to checking all the physical factors, we need to also double-check our spiritual relationships since the biblical passage we just noted promises rejuvenating sleep to the righteous.

Having mentioned a biological clock, it would probably be good to stop at this point for a quick explanation that each person's natural daily rhythm is unique to that individual person. However, there are some basic patterns that can generalize most of us. These patterns tend to fall into two major divisions: those people whom we often call "larks" because they function best in the early morning and those individuals whom we often label "owls" because they find themselves more energized later in the evening and even into the night. Let's compare what doctors have discovered about the daily ebb and flow of the mental energies of these two groups.

Morning Lark

5:30 AM	up
6-8 AM	creativity
8 AM-12:30 PM	problem solving
12:30-2:30 PM	bad time for concentration
2:30-4:30 PM	problem solving
4:30-8 PM	rejuvenation
8-10 PM	bad time for concentration
10 PM	bed

Night Owl

8 AM	up
8-10 AM	bad time for concentration
10 AM-noon	creativity
Noon-1 PM	problem solving
1-3 PM	bad time for concentration
3-6 PM	rejuvenation
6-11 PM	problem solving
11-midnight	bad time for concentration
Midnight	bed

Notice that both groups come out fairly equal in the amount of time relegated to each category. With most of the differences being only half an hour, the significance isn't in the quantity of time in each slot but the time of day at which each peak and slump occurs. The conclusion we can draw from this analysis is that being a lark or an owl is not better than the other – only different. By understanding this point, we can stop comparing ourselves with others and begin to work with our own inbuilt rhythm to optimize the God-given qualities inside us.

In addition to the many physical benefits our bodies gain from our sleep time, there are also many spiritual benefits associated with the down time our brains experience during sleep. A simple glance through the Bible will reveal a multitude of people who had life-changing inspirations and a number of others who had history-making revelations while asleep. One particularly interesting example is found in the story of Jacob who, after cheating his brother out of his birthright and inheritance, had a vision of angels ascending and descending a ladder stretched between earth and heaven. At the top of that staircase stood God Himself who appeared to assure the schemer that He had a good plan for his life and would guarantee His covenant promise regardless of how deceptive Jacob had been in obtaining the birthright and his father's blessing. (Genesis 28:10-15) When he awoke from his dream, Jacob made a stunning proclamation, *Surely the LORD is in this place; and I knew it not.* (Genesis 28:16) It was only in his sleep that Jacob could hear from God. His own evaluation of the situation was that he was totally unaware of the presence of God as long as he was awake.

Jacob's son Joseph followed in his father's pattern of hearing from God through dreams. Genesis chapter thirty-seven records two dreams that set the course of the young man's destiny – a destiny that involved not only his own dreams but also the dreams of others. Through interpreting the dreams of his prison mates and the dream of the king of Egypt, Joseph was propelled into the most pivotal position in the most powerful government of his time. This role allowed him to, in his own words, preserve the life of the nations. (Genesis 45:5)

Abraham, the forefather of these two dreamers, had a powerful dreamtime experience that confirmed his God-given covenant – a covenant that not only determined his personal destiny but also that of all his descendants, including not only Jacob and Joseph but every Jewish person who has ever trodden this earth's soil as well. That overwhelming night encounter was so potent in its nature that it struck terror throughout Abraham's being as it solidified a promise that has been under siege through every subsequent generation of history – even to the present day!

> *And when the sun was going down, a deep sleep fell upon Abram; and, lo, an horror of great darkness fell upon him. And he said unto Abram, Know of a surety that thy seed*

51

shall be a stranger in a land that is not theirs, and shall serve them; and they shall afflict them four hundred years; And also that nation, whom they shall serve, will I judge: and afterward shall they come out with great substance. And thou shalt go to thy fathers in peace; thou shalt be buried in a good old age. But in the fourth generation they shall come hither again: for the iniquity of the Amorites is not yet full. And it came to pass, that, when the sun went down, and it was dark, behold a smoking furnace, and a burning lamp that passed between those pieces. In the same day the LORD made a covenant with Abram, saying, Unto thy seed have I given this land, from the river of Egypt unto the great river, the river Euphrates: The Kenites, and the Kenizzites, and the Kadmonites, And the Hittites, and the Perizzites, and the Rephaims, And the Amorites, and the Canaanites, and the Girgashites, and the Jebusites. (Genesis 15:12-21)

Generations later, a young priestly assistant found it hard to sleep as he kept hearing a whisper calling his name. Finally, Samuel's mentor recognized that this beckoning was coming from God Himself and instructed the lad as to how to answer the divine call. The visitation that night set the immediate course for the next several generations and the pattern for the continued history of the nation of Israel. (I Samuel chapter three) Many generations still further into the course of time, God spoke through dreams and night visions to proclaim the future course and destiny of not only Israel but all the gentile nations as well – scenarios that are still being played out today with bulldozers in the Palestinian neighborhoods of East Jerusalem, slingshots in the Gaza Strip, suicide bombers at bus stops in Israel, and short- and medium-range missiles in the hands of Middle Eastern nations set on destroying the "Small

Satan" and her Western ally, the "Great Satan." (Daniel 1:17 and chapters two, four, five, seven, eight, and ten)

Other Old Testament characters whose life courses were determined through dreams include Abimelech (Genesis chapter twenty), Jacob and his uncle/double father-in-law Laban (Genesis chapter thirty-one), Gideon (Judges chapter seven), and King Solomon (I Kings chapter five). The New Testament opens with a flurry of dream activity as God speaks through dreams to direct Joseph not to be afraid to marry Mary and then gives direction to him and the Wise Men about steps they must take to ensure the baby Jesus' safety. (Matthew chapter two) God continued to use dreams as He attempted to warn Pilate about crucifying Christ (Matthew 27:19) and then to the Apostle Paul as he expanded the mission of the church to include the gentile nations (Acts 16:9, 19:9).

Let's back up just a bit to a point that I made just before we began looking at how God has used dreams to speak to men and direct their lives and even alter the course of history. By speaking of the brain's "down time," I made a statement that was not altogether factual. Actually, our brains do not become totally inactive during sleep. They use that time when we are not consciously active for a myriad of unconscious activities including reorganizing all the bits of information that we have received during the day. Much as a computer has to determine where it will store all the data that has been entered into its memory bank, our brains have to take some time to organize all the thoughts that they are expected to retain. How often have you heard someone who is in the process of trying to make an important decision use the expression, "Let me sleep on it"? What that person is saying is that he wants to take advantage of this subconscious mental operation so that he can see all the facts in a freshly organized perspective that may take into account bits of information that he may not have even been consciously aware of when he picked them up the previous day. I personally believe that God is actively involved in the lives of believers one hundred percent of the time. That means that He must also be actively involved in this nighttime subconscious brain activity as well. Therefore, He is actually in control of how our thoughts and memories get reorganized as we sleep. The result is that when we wake up each morning, we should have an enlightened perspective on everything that we have seen and heard the day before. In other words, even without a dream or night vision, we have actually heard from the Lord during our sleep! With this thought in mind, now we can understand why we often awaken in the morning with fresh thoughts and new ideas. My mentor, Dr. Lester Sumrall, always kept a pen and notebook next to the bed because he never wanted to miss a good thought that the Lord might drop into his heart during the night.

In my own personal life, I use the first thoughts I have when I awaken in the morning as a monitor of my own spiritual life. Generally, I awaken with the words to one of my favorite Christian songs cycling through my head. This is a great indication because we are admonished in scripture to meditate on psalms, hymns, and spiritual songs. (Ephesians 5:19; Colossians 3:16) However, I remember one particular occasion when I woke up for several mornings in a row with the words to a secular song echoing in my head. The lyrics were not lewd or perverted, but the song was not something that edified me or exalted the Lord. (I Corinthians 14:26) Therefore, I began to make a serious effort to renew my mind (Romans 12:2) so that I was more spiritually minded (Romans 8:6) during the day. The result was that I soon returned to my normal pattern of waking up with spiritual songs reverberating in my mind. In addition to songs, I often have ideas for new books or lessons, thoughts of how to accomplish projects that I have been working on, or individual's names in my first thoughts. When I contact the individuals whose names are in my first thoughts, almost without exception, those individuals are going through some very difficult time in their lives and really need a word of encouragement and prayer support. Isaiah described his own experience along these lines by saying:

The Lord GOD hath given me the tongue of the learned, that I should know how to speak a word in season to him that is weary: he wakeneth morning by morning, he wakeneth mine ear to hear as the learned. (Isaiah 50:4)

I am also certain that this sort of subconscious direction of our thoughts during sleep is what the psalmist was referring to when he spoke of the meditations on his bed during the night watches (Psalm 4:4, 63:6, 149:5) and what Solomon was referring to when he spoke of the working of the Word of God in our lives during our sleep (Proverbs 6:22). I wonder if this might be the reasoning behind the thrice-repeated command in the Song of Solomon that the lover not be awakened until he pleases; perhaps the maiden knew that Solomon needed to have his full nighttime communion with the Lord so that he would be at his best for his daytime activities. (Song of Solomon 2:7, 3:5, 5:2, 8:4)

Sleep is repeatedly referred to in the scripture as a blessing and is associated with many promises from God (Job 3:23; Psalm 3:5, 4:8, 139:18; Ecclesiastes 5:12; Jeremiah 31:26), and dreams are repeatedly spoken of as a chosen method for God to speak to and direct His people (Numbers 12:6, Joel 2:28, Acts 2:17); however, we must not forget that there are also many negative statements about sleep recorded in the Bible. Some men may point to the opening chapters of the Bible and suggest that if Adam had never fallen asleep (Genesis 2:21) he would not have wound up with Eve who, although she was initially a joyful addition to his life, eventually brought him a lot of trouble and pain. Well, be that argument as it may, there is certainly no question that Sisera should have never accepted Jael's offer of a cup of warm milk (Judges chapter four), that Samson certainly got into a lot of trouble when he fell asleep in the lap of Delilah (Judges chapter sixteen), that King Saul fell into serious jeopardy when he and all his body guards fell asleep (I Samuel chapter twenty-six), that Ishbosheth should have never taken a nap in the middle of the day (II Samuel chapter four), that all ten virgins should have stayed awake and kept their lamps full of oil (Matthew chapter twenty-five), and that Jesus' disciples should have been able to stay awake in the Garden of Gethsemane (Matthew chapter twenty-six). Additionally, the Lord has a lot to say about dreams and dreamers who may not be of Him. (Deuteronomy 13:1, 3, 5; Job 7:14, 20:8, 33:15-22; Ecclesiastes 5:3, 7; Jeremiah 23:25, 27, 28, 32, 27:9, 29:8; Zechariah 10:2; Jude 1:8) When God does make negative statements about sleep, the first focus seems to be on the amount of time that people sleep or the season during which they choose to sleep. (Proverbs 10:5, 19:15, 20:13) Solomon crystallized the whole issue of oversleeping in Proverbs 6:9-11 and then felt that the point was so significant that he repeated it again in chapter twenty-four:

> *How long wilt thou sleep, O sluggard? when wilt thou arise out of thy sleep? Yet a little sleep, a little slumber, a little folding of the hands to sleep: So shall thy poverty come as one that travelleth, and thy want as an armed man.*

Jesus' teachings confirm that during the unsuspecting hours of sleep, we might not only become subject to theft and vandalism but might also miss God's intended blessing. (Matthew 13:24-30, 24:42-44, 25:1-13; Luke 11:5-8, 17:34) The second area of concern seems to be on the attitudes of the people that would make them so drowsy. (Psalm 76:5, Hosea 7:6, Romans 11:8) Perhaps the most significant of the Lord's concerns is that it is those men and women He has called to be the most attentive and watchful who are prone to fall into stupefying slumber. (Isaiah 29:10, 56:10; Nahum 3:18) At the very moment when Jesus was ready to give His inner circle their most incredible revelation of His glory, they fell asleep; fortunately, they awoke just in time to experience the Lord's transfiguration and the visitation of the two Old Testament saints. (Luke 9:28-36)

Having noted that the scriptures speak of not only the positive aspects of sleep but also the negative result of oversleeping, let's take a quick look at some studies concerning the duration of natural sleep. A recent study found that people today sleep one and a half hours less per night than our ancestors did a century ago. In fact, the tendency toward less sleep is continually increasing. A 2008 study found that only twenty-eight percent of the subjects reported getting eight hours of sleep each night, down ten percentage points from the number reported in a 2001 poll. This lack of sufficient sleep is taking a toll on modern society. Insufficient sleep over time has been linked to depression, decreased cognitive performance, immune suppression, blood sugar imbalance, and even obesity. Teens with inadequate sleep tend to have higher than normal levels of rage, depression, drug and alcohol abuse, auto accidents, and low grades. Even one night of poor sleep can cause fatigue, memory loss, and decreased mental capacity. Since going for twenty hours without sleep can put an individual in the same state of mental disorientation as if he had a .08 blood-alcohol content, it is no wonder that drowsy drivers are responsible for fifteen hundred traffic deaths and seventy-one thousand injures each year.

On the other hand, scientific studies also indicate that oversleeping can be just as detrimental as undersleeping. Using eight hours of sleep per night as the norm, it was discovered that men who add an extra hour actually increase their chances of dying within the next ten-year period by nineteen percent. Women who increase their sleep by an hour also increase their chances of dying within the next ten years by a whopping thirty-five percent. Extend that increased sleep pattern by yet an additional hour and the odds of dying within the next ten years jump up to seventy-five percent for men and one hundred twelve percent for women! With numbers like this at stake, it is no wonder the scriptures contain at least a dozen commands to wake up! (Judges 5:12; I Kings 19:5; Isaiah 51:9, 17, 52:1; Jonah 1:6; Zechariah 4:1; Matthew 1:24, Romans 13:11; I Corinthians 15:34; Ephesians 5:14, I Thessalonians 5:6) It is also interesting that death is referred to as sleep at least fifty-five times in the scripture. (Deuteronomy 31:16; II Samuel 7:12; I Kings 1:21, 2:10, 11:21, 11:43, 14:20, 14:31, 15:8, 16:6, 16:28, 22:40, 22:50; II Kings 4:31, 8:24, 10:35, 13:9, 13:13, 14:16, 14:22, 15:38, 16:20, 20:21, 21:18, 24:6; II Chronicles 9:31, 12:16, 14:1, 1:13, 21:1, 26:27, 32:33, 33:20; Job 7:21, 14:12, 20:8; Psalm 13:3, 17:15, 76:6; Isaiah 26:19; Jeremiah 51:39, 51:57; Daniel 12:2; Matthew 9:24, 27:52; Mark 5:39; Luke 8:52; John 11:11-13; Acts 13:36; I Corinthians 11:30, 15:20, 15:51; Ephesians 5:14; I Thessalonians 4:14, 5:10) Is it possible that there is more than just a metaphor at play here? Is it possible that God is actually building on the connection between oversleeping and physical death?

Whether it is waking up from a normal sleeping period in which the Lord has refreshed our inner man while the rest has refreshed our physical man or whether it is being aroused out of lethargically excessive sleep or possibly even a night when we find it impossible to fall asleep (Esther 6:1), the real value of life comes with how we function once we have shaken ourselves and taken on the day at hand. Think back to some of the men who received God's directions through dreams. Had Jacob not acted on the dream instructing him as to how to breed his flocks, he would have never prospered enough to be released from servitude to Laban. Had Pharaoh not relentlessly pursued finding someone to interpret his dream, the nation would have starved during the seven years of famine and he would not have become the wealthiest monarch on earth. Had Joseph not responded to the angelic visitation in his dream, the whole Christmas story would read differently because Mary would not have been part of his family and, therefore, would never have gone to Bethlehem and given birth to the Christ child in the manger of the "overflow" suite at the local inn.

One inventor friend of mine testifies that a number of his inventions came to him during his sleep as a result of committing his projects to the Lord in prayer after having spent many waking hours fruitlessly seeking for a way to make them work. Getting the revelation was one thing, but taking the idea into the laboratory and actually putting it through the litmus test of building and testing a prototype was the "proof of the pudding." So it is with our spiritual lives as well; when we wake up each morning, we must step out of bed with a determination to follow the promptings we have received either through our God-given dreams or from the renewed thoughts that He drops into our refreshed minds. Just take a minute to meditate on a few of the passages that equate being awake with becoming diligently involved in God's plans.

> *Awake up, my glory; awake, psaltery and harp: I myself will awake early.* (Psalm 57:8)
> *I will not give sleep to mine eyes, or slumber to mine eyelids, Until I find out a place for the LORD, an habitation for the mighty God of Jacob.* (Psalm 132:4-5)
> *Give not sleep to thine eyes, nor slumber to thine eyelids. Deliver thyself as a roe from the hand of the hunter, and as a bird from the hand of the fowler.* (Proverbs 6:4-5)
> *Watch ye therefore: for ye know not when the master of the house cometh, at even, or at midnight, or at the cockcrowing, or in the morning: Lest coming suddenly he find you sleeping. And what I say unto you I say unto all, Watch.* (Mark 13:36)
> *And he cometh, and findeth them sleeping, and saith unto Peter, Simon, sleepest thou? couldest not thou watch one hour?* (Mark 14:37, see also Luke 22:45-46)
> *Therefore let us not sleep, as do others; but let us watch and be sober. For they that sleep sleep in the night; and they that be drunken are drunken in the night.* (I Thessalonians 5:7)

By this point, we have certainly come to the understanding that both sleeping and waking have their unique benefits and that both are needed in our physical and spiritual lives. One of God's primary principles in scripture is the balance between work and rest. In fact, when He instituted the weekly day of rest and sabbatical year, He even made it a capital crime to violate His rhythm of work and rest. (Exodus 23:11, 23:12, 31:15, 34:21, 35:2; Leviticus 23:3, 16:31, 23:32, 25:4, 25:5; Deuteronomy 5:14) The scriptures that promise us seasons of rest and show that God has been active in fulfilling His promise are too numerous to mention (Exodus 33:14; Deuteronomy 3:20, 12:9, 12:10, 25:19; Joshua 1:13, 1:15, 21:44, 22:4, 23:1; Judges 3:11, 3:30, 5:31; Ruth 1:9, 3:1; II Samuel 7:1, 7:11; I Kings 5:4, 8:56; I Chronicles 22:9, 22:18, 23:25; II Chronicles 14:6, 14:7, 15:15, 20:30; Esther 9:16; Job 3:13, 3:17, 3:18, 11:18, 14:6, 17:16; Psalms 16:9, 37:7, 55:6, 94:13, 116:7, 132:14; Isaiah 14:3, 14:7, 28:12, 30:15, 57:2, 63:14; Jeremiah 6:16, 30:10, 31:2, 46:27, 50:34; Zechariah 1:11; Matthew 11:28, 11:29; Mark 6:31; Acts 2:26; II Thessalonians 1:7, Hebrews 4:1-11; Revelation 6:11, 14:13), yet we see a stark warning in the case of the tribe of Issachar who wound up in slavery because they became complacent and refused to get back up and go forward with the task at hand when they found rest from their burdens (Genesis 49:15). Jesus gave us a parable that seems to make the point that rest and work must go hand in hand if we are to see the kingdom of God manifest in our lives:

> *And he said, So is the kingdom of God, as if a man should cast seed into the ground; And should sleep, and rise night and day, and the seed should spring and grow up, he knoweth not how. For the earth bringeth forth fruit of herself; first the blade, then the ear, after that the full corn in the ear. But when the fruit is brought forth, immediately he putteth in the sickle, because the harvest is come.* (Mark 4:26-29)

Notice that in this illustration of the kingdom, the farmer both slept and rose up during the process of producing his crop. So it is with our spiritual lives – we must learn how to balance the rejuvenating time necessary to build up our spiritual lives with the alert, active time when we are attentive to aggressively building the kingdom. Paul's admonition to the church in Ephesians 5:14 is that we awake and arise from the dead, indicating that the sleep we are to abandon is the lethargic, death-like oversleeping that cripples us and renders us useless to the kingdom – not the rejuvenating well-balanced sleep necessary for our spiritual health.

Two well-loved passages – one from the Old Testament and one from the New – present this harmonious balance between restful rejuvenation and attentive alertness. Notice how the twenty-third Psalm juxtapositions lying down in the green pastures for the restoration of the soul with being led in the paths of righteousness and how Jesus' famous call to the laborers and the heavy laden couples receiving His rest with taking up His yoke.

> *The LORD is my shepherd; I shall not want.*
> *He maketh me to lie down in green pastures:*
> *he leadeth me beside the still waters. He*
> *restoreth my soul: he leadeth me in the paths*
> *of righteousness for his name's sake.* (Psalm
> 23:1-3)
> *Come unto me, all ye that labour and are*
> *heavy laden, and I will give you rest. Take*
> *my yoke upon you, and learn of me; for I am*
> *meek and lowly in heart: and ye shall find*
> *rest unto your souls. For my yoke is easy,*
> *and my burden is light.* (Matthew 11:28-30)

Paul's wake-up call to the church culminates with the proclamation that, when we respond to Christ, He will give us light – a promise that certainly reaches much further than most of us might ever imagine. To begin to grasp what he might have been trying to communicate, let's think back to the very beginning when light was the first thing on God's creative agenda. (Genesis 1:3) How often do we recite that powerful verse, *Let there be light!* without even giving a second thought as to how significant it is that light was the first order of creation. Without light, none of the other elements of creation would have been functional. Light is the primary source of energy in the universe. The energy of sunlight causes plants to grow and weather patterns to develop. Without plant life, there would be no fossil fuels to power our modern machinery, no oxygen to breathe, and no food for animals or humans. Without weather patterns, there would be no rain or snow to distribute the moisture through the planet, rendering only the coastal regions habitable. Without rain, there would be no rivers to produce hydroelectric energy for powering the cities. Without weather patterns of wind and currents, there would be no distribution of seeds, resulting in only isolated spots of vegetation. Most significantly, without light, there would be no warmth – yielding only a barren wasteland of nothingness.

The necessity of light is demonstrated in the story of the plagues that God leveled against Egypt as Pharaoh refused to let His people go. As the level of devastation intensified with each plague, Moses neared his ultimate catastrophe as he called the ninth of ten calamities upon the resistant ruler – darkness. Yet, as a sign of His sovereignty and mercy upon His own people, God ensured that the Israelites had light while the Egyptians groped in debilitating darkness. (Exodus 10:23) It is also significant that when the Israelites did make their way out of Egypt that they were led by a pillar that manifested itself as a cloud during the daytime but as a fire of light each night. (Exodus 13:21, 14:20) When God directed the people to build a place of worship for Him, one of the most noteworthy elements was the perpetual light from the eternal flame on the candlestick that was to never be allowed to flicker out. (Exodus 25:37, 27:20; Leviticus 24:2)

But the real question is not about how significant light is; rather, it has to do with why light is so significant. It seems that the simple explanation is that light actually represents God Himself. The psalmist proclaimed, *The LORD is my light and my salvation; whom shall I fear? the LORD is the strength of my life; of whom shall I be afraid?* (Psalm 27:1) and the prophet declared, *The sun shall be no more thy light by day; neither for brightness shall the moon give light unto thee: but the LORD shall be unto thee an everlasting light, and thy God thy glory.* (Isaiah 60:19) The New Testament is even more demonstrative that Jesus is the light.

> *In him was life; and the life was the light of men. And the light shineth in darkness; and the darkness comprehended it not...The same came for a witness, to bear witness of the Light, that all men through him might believe...That was the true Light, which lighteth every man that cometh into the world...And this is the condemnation, that light is come into the world, and men loved darkness rather than light, because their deeds were evil...Then spake Jesus again unto them, saying, I am the light of the world: he that followeth me shall not walk in darkness, but shall have the light of life...As long as I am in the world, I am the light of the world...I am come a light into the world, that whosoever believeth on me should not abide in darkness.* (John 1:4, 1:5, 1:7, 1:9, 3:19, 8:12, 9:5, 12:46. See also Acts 9:3, 12:7, 13:47, 22:6, 22:11, 26:13; I Timothy 6:16; I John 1:5; Revelation 21:23, 22:5)

The wonderful reality is that these are not just theological principles, but life-changing truths in that God has promised to flood us with this divine light so that we can live and walk in His very presence.

> *For thou wilt light my candle: the LORD my God will enlighten my darkness.* (Psalm 18:28)
> *Blessed is the people that know the joyful sound: they shall walk, O LORD, in the light of thy countenance.* (Psalm 89:15)

But the path of the just is as the shining light, that shineth more and more unto the perfect day. (Proverbs 4:18)
O house of Jacob, come ye, and let us walk in the light of the LORD. (Isaiah 2:5)
Then Jesus said unto them, Yet a little while is the light with you. Walk while ye have the light, lest darkness come upon you: for he that walketh in darkness knoweth not whither he goeth. (John 12:35)
But if we walk in the light, as he is in the light, we have fellowship one with another, and the blood of Jesus Christ his Son cleanseth us from all sin. (I John 1:7. See also Psalm 104:2, 43:3, 112:4, 118:27)

But the really astonishing revelation is that not only are we promised to have the benefits of the light of God, we are also invited to actually become that light in our present world. Many occult and spiritualist groups misinterpret this concept to say that we are little deities; however, this is not at all what the scriptures are intending to teach us. Rather, we are to emit the light of God who is inside us to the point that when the world around us looks at our lives, they are able to see the God who indwells us. In the same way that Genesis refers to the moon as a light (Genesis 1:16) when actually it is not a source of light itself but a reflection of the sun's light, we are not lights in our own right but conduits for the light of God who is inside us. (Galatians 2:20)

Ye are the light of the world. A city that is set on an hill cannot be hid. Neither do men light a candle, and put it under a bushel, but on a candlestick; and it giveth light unto all that are in the house. Let your light so shine before men, that they may see your good works, and glorify your Father which is in heaven. (Matthew 5:14-16)
Ye are all the children of light, and the

*children of the day: we are not of the night,
nor of darkness.* (I Thessalonians 5:5)
*But ye are a chosen generation, a royal
priesthood, an holy nation, a peculiar
people; that ye should shew forth the praises
of him who hath called you out of darkness
into his marvellous light.* (I Peter 2:9. See
also Isaiah 42:6, 49:6, 60:1, 60:3; Luke 8:16,
11:33)

What should we anticipate as the result of our awaking
from our God-ordained time of spiritual restoration to the
realization that we are God's light bulbs in our present society?
(See also Isaiah 42:6, 49:6, 60:1, 60:3; Luke 8:16, 11:33) First
of all, it would seem that since the Word of God is considered
God's light for our lives (Psalm 119:105, 130), we would
become people of the Word. Psalm 1:2 describes a righteous
man as one who meditates on the law of the Lord both day and
night. The next characteristic of a person who is filled with the
light of God is that he should become an automatic witness to
the unbelievers around him. We have already noted Jesus'
words about letting our light shine from the candlestick rather
than hiding it under a basket, but this is only one of many
passages from both the New and Old Testaments revealing
God's plan for all people to see His light shine into their dark
worlds. (Isaiah 9:2; Matthew 4:16; Luke 1:79, 2:32; Acts
26:18, 26:23; II Corinthians 4:6) In fact, this was the whole
context into which the apostle introduced his spiritual wake-up
call.

*For ye were sometimes darkness, but now
are ye light in the Lord: walk as children of
light.* (Ephesians 5:8)

Additionally, the people who are beacons of the light of
Christ will find themselves walking in superhuman love and
forgiveness for his Christian brother. (I John 2:8-10) In that
Isaiah 58:8 associates light with healing, we must conclude that
people who are filled with the light of Christ would be people

of healing. Indeed, Jesus repeatedly told us that our mission was to heal the sick. (Matthew 10:7-9; Mark 16:15-18; Luke 9:1-3, 10:8-10) Additionally, through the light of God's wisdom and insight, we should be people who are able to discern the heart of issues and to see the underlying elements that would be hidden from those who observe things with only their natural understanding (I Corinthians 4:5, Ephesians 5:13) or have even been blinded by Satan, the god of the present world order. (John 9:39-41, II Corinthians 4:4)

Unfortunately, many believers are falling far short of the God-given privileges and authority afforded us as children of light. (Luke 16:8) Therefore, we must ask the Holy Spirit to reveal inside us what are the inheritance promises conveyed to us as children of light (Colossians 1:12), and then – taking up the spiritual weaponry which only the children of light can wield (Romans 13:12) – we must aggressively contend until we see the fulfillment of the eschatological promise that the light of God's salvation will shine among all the nations.

And the nations of them which are saved shall walk in the light of it: and the kings of the earth do bring their glory and honour into it. (Revelation 21:24)

Chapter Three
Everything You Need to Know
is in Chapter Three Verse Sixteen

Several years ago, when I ran across a book entitled Everything I Need to Know, I Learned in Kindergarten, I knew that I was in trouble since I never went to kindergarten. However, I have since come to realize that everything I really needed to know, I learned by reading chapter three, verse sixteen.

By reading John 3:16, *For God so loved the world, that he gave his only begotten Son, that whosoever believeth in him should not perish, but have everlasting life,* I learned a number of important lessons about salvation:

1) There is a God.
2) He loves – not hates – me.
3) Jesus is His son.
4) I have a choice to make.
5) Depending on what choice I make, I will either perish or inherit eternal life.

Next, I turned to Luke 3:16, *John answered, saying unto them all, I indeed baptize you with water; but one mightier than I cometh, the latchet of whose shoes I am not worthy to unloose: he shall baptize you with the Holy Ghost and with fire,* where I learned some important principles about baptism in water and the baptism in the Holy Spirit:

1) Water baptism is a requirement of the Christian faith.
2) Holy Ghost baptism is necessary for the Christian life.
3) Sanctification (the baptism of fire) is essential for Christian holiness.

From Acts 3:16, *And his name through faith in his name hath made this man strong, whom ye see and know: yea, the faith which is by him hath given him this perfect soundness in the presence of you all*, I gained some pertinent truths about healing:

1) Physical, as well as spiritual, healing is available.
2) Faith is the key to receiving physical healing.
3) It is only through the name and authority of Jesus that we can experience miraculous healing and deliverance.

By turning to II Timothy 3:16, *All scripture is given by inspiration of God, and is profitable for doctrine, for reproof, for correction, for instruction in righteousness*, I received a new revelation on the inspiration of scripture:

1) The Word of God is inerrant.
2) It is important for us, in such uncertain times, to have something in life that is certain.
3) The inerrant Word must benefit me and have an effect on my life that brings me to a place of change and where the errors in my life can be dealt with.

In flipping to the end of the Book and reading Revelation 3:16, *So then because thou art lukewarm, and neither cold nor hot, I will spue thee out of my mouth*, I learned an important lesson about being lukewarm:

The Christian life is the "real deal" and it cannot be taken half-heartedly or nonchalantly.

In I Corinthians 3:16, *Know ye not that ye are the temple of God, and that the Spirit of God dwelleth in you?* I was confronted with some powerful truths about seeing myself as the very temple of the Holy Spirit:

1) I'm not trash; I'm God's habitation.
2) I'd better change the way I act to reflect my noble

position.

3) I'd better think more positively about myself since God Himself considers me worthy to be His habitation.

James 3:16, *For where envying and strife is, there is confusion and every evil work*, helped me to understand something about envy:

> If I'm not careful about how I feel toward others, I can get myself into an awful fix with every evil work operating in my life.

It was in I John 3:16, *Hereby perceive we the love of God, because he laid down his life for us: and we ought to lay down our lives for the brethren*, that I learned about unselfish giving:

> Christianity isn't just receiving; it's really about giving.

Finally, in II Thessalonians 3:16, *Now the Lord of peace himself give you peace always by all means. The Lord be with you all*, I came to know several important truths about peace in my Christian life:

1) God is a God of peace.
2) He is willing to give me His peace.
3) If I'm not living in peace, I'm certainly not living in the fullness of Christ's provisions and possibly not living in Him at all.

I'm sure that I missed a lot by not getting to go to kindergarten, but I'm thankful that I did get to go to chapter three, verse sixteen!

Chapter Four
Colossal Colossians

The Colossus of Rhodes towered more than one hundred feet above the harbor of the Greek island of Rhodes, making it one of the tallest statues of the ancient world. This gigantic statue of the Greek god Helios was erected about three hundred years before the birth of Christ and was considered one of the Seven Wonders of the Ancient World. After its collapse due to earthquake damage, it took nine hundred camels to haul off the scrap metal.

The English language has adapted the term "colossal" from this monstrous work of art to speak of things of outstanding proportions. Even though Colossians is actually one of the smaller of Paul's epistles, this little volume seems to deserve the title "colossal" since it packs a mighty theological punch and weighs in as one of the most significant treatments of who Christ is in us and who we are in Him.

If this were a Bible college or seminary text, we would have to begin our study with a certain number of essential facts that many of us would find boring as we impatiently mutter under our breath, "Let's get on with the good stuff. I want to learn what's actually in the book, not a bunch of facts surrounding the book." Well, try to be a bit forgiving as I take the first few lines to deal with these boring facts. Scholars believe that Colossians was written by the Apostle Paul around 60-62 AD from a prison cell in Rome. It has been widely noted that there is a very close parallel between this letter and the one to the Ephesians. Furthermore, many Bible teachers speculate that the letter to the Ephesians was not actually directed to the Ephesian church specifically; rather, they suggest that it is more likely to have been a circular letter that was intended to be read by all the churches in Asia Minor, which is modern-day Turkey. The very earliest copies of the letter to the Ephesians did not bear this title; they simply were not addressed to anyone at all. This lack of a title, along with the general terminology used throughout the book has led many scholars to conclude that Paul had intended it for a much wider audience than just one church. When compared to the way most of his letters give point-blank advice to specific issues in the churches, it is readily observable that the Ephesian letter has a rather unique, generalized tone.

But wait – we are studying Colossians, not Ephesians. Well, if we take a little time to consider the full discussion, the significance of these thoughts will eventually become clear. Well, back to Ephesians – it is likely that the copies that do say "Ephesians" were from the copy of the circular letter that was actually sent to that specific city, while other copies went to other churches in the same general area, perhaps the seven churches of Asia Minor mentioned in Revelation chapters two and three. Now, to explain why it is necessary to discuss Ephesians in order to understand Colossians: even a cursory overview of the two letters reveals that Colossians is very similar to Ephesians. This similarity has led Bible students to surmise that it is likely that the two were written at about the same time and may have even been based on the same outline – at least the same mental outline, if not the same physical outline. Based on references in Colossians about another letter that had been sent to the Laodicean church, some scholars have gone so far as to suggest that Colossians was also a circular letter that was to be passed between the two churches of Colosse and Laodicea, if not all the churches in Asia Minor. It is an intriguing idea to consider that this "Laodicean letter" may have even been the untitled version of the letter we now know as Ephesians.

Now that we have dragged our way through all these scholarly facts, it's time to discuss their significance. In doing so, I suspect that we'll discover that these facts aren't all that boring after all. If the suggested date and place of writing are correct, then Colossians is one of the last works of the Apostle Paul. It is commonly held that Paul was martyred in Rome around 67 AD. This chronology places the letter during the last five years or so of his life, meaning that this letter gives us the full benefit of his total spiritual maturity. I know that it is almost automatic for us to assume that Paul was instantly matured the moment he met Jesus on the road to Damascus, but we really need to stop and remember that he was still a human, no matter how dramatic his encounter with the risen Christ. Just one quick example of his maturing process can be seen in the seventeenth and eighteenth chapters of Acts. In chapter seventeen, we find the apostle in Athens debating with the philosophers on Mars Hill. No matter how eloquent his presentation was, it yielded almost no fruit. The concluding verse of this chapter suggests that only a handful of followers resulted from his ministry there – certainly not the revival that usually flared up wherever he landed. In the eighteenth chapter, he moved on to Corinth where he was able to establish a flourishing church. In his first letter back to that church, he tells us about his approach in this particular city, *And I, brethren, when I came to you, came not with excellency of speech or of wisdom, declaring unto you the testimony of God. For I determined not to know any thing among you, save Jesus Christ, and him crucified. And I was with you in weakness, and in fear, and in much trembling. And my speech and my preaching was not with enticing words of man's wisdom, but in demonstration of the Spirit and of power: That your faith should not stand in the wisdom of men, but in the power of God.* Essentially, what he was saying was that he had abandoned the approach he had used in Athens and had adopted a different technique with them. He had matured in his ministry between leaving Athens and his arrival in Corinth. If he had changed so significantly on that short journey, imagine how much more seasoned he must have been by the time he came to those last few years and stood poised at the very portal of heaven.

If the letter was indeed a circular letter, there is a certain richness to it that will not be found in the more where-the-rubber-meets-the-road letters like the Corinthian epistles and the letter to the Galatians. In these letters, he offers more practical counsel concerning specific issues. In the Corinthian correspondence, for example, the church members had sent him a list of questions that he enumerates and then addresses. (I Corinthians 7:1-16:18) In the Colossian letter, he is not addressing any specific issues; therefore, he is able to give in-depth revelation concerning the issue – who Christ is in us and who we are in Him! Furthermore, if indeed this correspondence is a circular letter that is associated with Ephesus and Laodicea, we have a parallel with the book of Revelation. Ephesus was the first church addressed, and Laodecia was the last. A further parallel can be seen with the depiction of the Risen Lord given in the Revelation as the Alpha and Omega, the First and the Last. The fact that the letter was for more than one church parallels with the message of the Revelation, *Let him who has an ear hear what the Spirit says to the churches.* Notice that the point is repeatedly made that the message is to be heard by all the churches, not just a specific one. It is a message of all-encompassing importance: Jesus is the author and the finisher of our faith.

The New Testament is not a theology book, although it is the only reliable book on theology. When I say that it is not a theology book, I am intending to say that it is not a systematic study of theology. Rather, it is a book of applied theology; it is a practical application of theology to the everyday problems of life. For example, Paul did not write the book of Galatians to impart theological lessons to the believers in Galatia but to correct errors and misconceptions in their church. In doing so, he had to explain a lot of theology along the way. The only letter that he wrote as a theological statement was the epistle to the Romans. This church was not one he had founded; in fact, it was not one he had even visited. Since he was not involved in their lives like he was in the other churches, he could not speak to them in the corrective tone with which he addressed the other churches. To the Romans, he imparted his spiritual gift of teaching in a more methodical manner by laying out a systematic explanation of the theology of salvation. Interestingly enough, he gave a condensed version of this same theology in the book of Ephesians and an even more condensed synopsis in the letter to the Colossians.

One interesting observation about the synopsis as recorded in Colossians is that the apostle does not mention the wrestling with spiritual principalities as he does in Ephesians chapter six. Is there a reason why? It seems clear that a truly spiritual believer should not have to be taught how to wrestle since our real position is one of authority over the forces of the enemy. As Dr. Lester Sumrall used to say, "Flies don't land on hot stoves." It is only by understanding the "boring facts" about the association between the letter to the Ephesians and the letter to the Colossians, that we are even aware of the lack of emphasis on the concept of spiritual warfare – and, therefore, are able to see where the true emphasis of the letter lies. Without seeing the parallel and the omitted emphasis, we could have missed the whole point of the letter. Obviously, we would have seen the fact that we are in great positions of authority through Christ, but it is likely that we would never have noticed his implication that the struggle is over!

In order to analyze the message of the book of Colossians, I'd like to consider six little words that embody the full content of the epistle. These words serve as acrostics that take us through literally every verse and idea in the book.

In the first chapter of the letter, Paul incorporates "The Christ Hymn" (verses fourteen through twenty), a section of scripture that most scholars assume to be a pre-existing creed that Paul saw as a crystallization of who the church saw Christ to be. Using this pre-existing creed or hymn would not be considered inappropriate or plagiarism any more than if you or I quoted from "Amazing Grace" or the Twenty-third Psalm in one of our speeches or sermons. However, I would like to take a minute to remember that poetry was not outside Paul's abilities. After all, no one has ever questioned that he penned the magnificent words on love in First Corinthians chapter thirteen. Regardless of whether Paul borrowed an existing hymn or composed his own, this section of the epistle epitomizes the revelation of the Risen Christ. By going through each of the letters in the word "Christ," we will discover all the characteristics attributed to Him in this hymn.

C stands for Creator, an attribute that depicts the divinity of the Eternal Christ. This concept is proclaimed in verse sixteen of chapter one, *For by him were all things created, that are in heaven, and that are in earth, visible and invisible, whether they be thrones, or dominions, or principalities, or powers: all things were created by him, and for him.* There are some interesting messages that are proclaimed in scripture, simply by their parallel structure. For instance, notice the parallelisms between Genesis 1:1, *In the beginning God created the heaven and the earth*, and John 1:1, *In the beginning was the Word, and the Word was with God, and the Word was God.* The parallel use of the idea of the beginning in these two verses leads to the understanding that John saw Jesus as equal to God, the Creator. In the book of Revelation, John uses another parallel structure to again show that he saw Jesus as equal to God, the Creator. In verse eleven of chapter four, he records a song of praise sung to the Father extolling Him as Creator, *Thou art worthy, O Lord, to receive glory and honour and power: for thou hast created all things, and for thy pleasure they are and were created.* Chapter five verse twelve presents a parallel accolade offered to Jesus, the Redeemer, *Worthy is the Lamb that was slain to receive power, and riches, and wisdom, and strength, and honour, and glory, and blessing.* The basic principle we all learned in Logic 101, "If A is equal to B and B is equal to C, then A is equal to C," definitely applies here: Jesus is equal to God because both are called the Creator. A further note on this verse is that it sets the stage for the idea that we have authority over our spiritual foes since they are nothing more than created entities who were made by Jesus – and <u>for</u> Him. Since they were created by Him, they are not His equal, and certainly not a viable threat to His kingdom. In that they were created for Him, it is unquestionable that they are not going to ultimately disgrace Him or His kingdom.

The **H** stands for Christ's position as **H**ead of the Church that depicts the authority of the Reigning Christ. This truth is proclaimed in chapter one verse eighteen, *And he is the head of the body, the church: who is the beginning, the* *firstborn from the dead; that in all things he might have the preeminence.* Parallel thoughts are found throughout the New Testament, but allow it to suffice that we mention only these few:, *And he gave some, apostles; and some, prophets; and some, evangelists; and some, pastors and teachers; For the perfecting of the saints, for the work of the ministry, for the edifying of the body of Christ: Till we all come in the unity of the faith, and of the knowledge of the Son of God, unto a perfect man, unto the measure of the stature of the fulness of Christ: That we henceforth be no more children, tossed to and fro, and carried about with every wind of doctrine, by the sleight of men, and cunning craftiness, whereby they lie in wait to deceive; But speaking the truth in love, may grow up into him in all things, which is the head, even Christ* (Ephesians 4:11-15), *For the husband is the head of the wife, even as Christ is the head of the church: and he is the saviour of the body* (Ephesians 5:23), and *But I would have you know, that the head of every man is Christ; and the head of the woman is the man; and the head of Christ is God* (I Corinthians 11:3).

The dramatic results of a recent poll showed that seventy percent of younger Christians and fifty-seven percent of the overall church answered that many religions lead to eternal life. However, when a follow-up study rephrased the question to make a distinction between religions other than Christianity and denominational affiliation, only thirty-one percent agreed. That still means that almost one out of every three of us believes that people can still get to heaven without accepting Jesus!! No wonder the church is so powerless in so many areas; we have abandoned the keynote principle of our faith: that Jesus – not Buddha, Vishnu, Joseph Smith, or even a consortium of all the great religious leaders of history – is the victorious head of the church!

R is for **Redeemer**, depicting the mission of the Suffering Christ. *In whom we have redemption through his blood, even the forgiveness of sins.* (verse 1:14) According to I John 3:8, the whole purpose that Christ was manifested in human flesh was to destroy the works of the devil. He did this by redeeming mankind from the fallen state that Satan had brought them into. We have already taken a brief look at the song of exaltation in Revelation 5:9-10, but it might be worthwhile to take the time to read it in its entirety here to see exactly what made Jesus worthy of the praises lavished upon Him, *Thou art worthy to take the book, and to open the seals thereof: for thou wast slain, and hast redeemed us to God by thy blood out of every kindred, and tongue, and people, and nation; And hast made us unto our God kings and priests: and we shall reign on the earth.* He is worthy because He has redeemed mankind – He has fulfilled His redemptive mission on the planet. Revelation 13:8 goes on to say, *And all that dwell upon the earth shall worship him, whose names are not written in the book of life of the Lamb slain from the foundation of the world.* Here again is reaffirmation that the redemptive work of His sacrificial death and victorious resurrection is what makes Him worthy of praise. This verse proclaims that Jesus was the Lamb slain from the foundation of the earth. If we were to go all the way back to the time of Adam and Eve's sin in the Garden of Eden (Genesis 3:15), we would discover that since "day one" this redemptive work has been intimately intermeshed with God's plan to redeem His fallen creation. As a – no, the – major theme of the Old Testament, the message of Christ's vicarious death is woven like a scarlet thread throughout the Jewish law, prophets, and writings. Two passages that unmistakably depict the crucifixion as the predetermined plan for redemption are Psalm 22:1-31, written a thousand years before the event, yet accurate to the most minute detail; and Isaiah 52:13-53:12, written some seven hundred years prior to the crucifixion yet totally precise in its depiction of not only the details but also the purpose of Jesus' death, *Surely he hath borne our griefs, and carried our sorrows: yet we did esteem him stricken, smitten of God, and afflicted. But he was wounded for our transgressions, he was bruised for our iniquities: the chastisement of our peace was upon him; and with his stripes we are healed...because he hath poured out his soul unto death: and he was numbered with the transgressors; and he bare the sin of many, and made intercession for the transgressors.*

I stands for the **I**mage of God, depicting the Identity of the Present Christ. Verse fifteen reads, *Who is the image of the invisible God, the firstborn of every creature.* The author of Hebrews expands on this theme, when he writes, *Who being the brightness of his glory, and the express image of his person, and upholding all things by the word of his power, when he had by himself purged our sins, sat down on the right hand of the Majesty on high.* (verse 1:3) In other words, the only way we will be able to see the invisible God is to behold Him in the person of Jesus Christ, exactly what Jesus Himself said when the disciples asked Him to show them the Father, *Have I been so long time with you, and yet hast thou not known me, Philip? he that hath seen me hath seen the Father; and how sayest thou then, Shew us the Father?* (John 14:9) Perhaps this is why God has always been so adamant in His hatred for idolatry and His command that there not be any images made to depict Him – He wanted our only revelation of Him to be in the person of Christ, who would not only be a wise teacher, miraculous healer, and victorious conqueror, but also a suffering sacrifice and a humble servant all at the same time. The fact that Jesus is the only true source of revelation of the Father is actually repeated twice in the hymn. In verse nineteen Paul adds, *For in him dwelleth all the fulness of the Godhead bodily.*

The **S** in "Christ" represents Sustainer, a depiction of the necessity of the Living Christ. In verse seventeen, Paul writes, *And he is before all things, and by him all things consist.* He is the glue that holds creation together. Without Him, our whole universe would either explode or implode. This is especially true of our own "personal universes." When Christ is left out of our lives, they immediately disintegrate into the nothingness of despair, hopelessness, misdirection, and self-destruction. In his message on Mars Hill in Athens, Paul alluded to this truth when he said, *For in him we live, and move, and have our being; as certain also of your own poets have said, For we are also his offspring.* (Acts 17:28) He continued to reaffirm this principle as he wrote to the churches under his care, *But to us there is but one God, the Father, of* *whom are all things, and we in him; and one Lord Jesus Christ, by whom are all things, and we by him* (I Corinthians 8:6), *For all the promises of God in him are yea, and in him Amen, unto the glory of God by us* (II Corinthians 1:20), *That in the dispensation of the fulness of times he might gather together in one all things in Christ, both which are in heaven, and which are on earth; even in him* (Ephesians 1:10), *There is one body, and one Spirit, even as ye are called in one hope of your calling; One Lord, one faith, one baptism, One God and Father of all, who is above all, and through all, and in you all. But unto every one of us is given grace according to the measure of the gift of Christ* (Ephesians 4:4-7). Perhaps that last verse sums it up most appropriately: Christ is above all, through all, and in all – Christ is all; without Him there is nothing!

T stands for the **T**otality of Everything that depicts the victory of the Risen Christ, a theme that is closely related to the last thought and also to the idea that He is the image of God. In verse nineteen, Paul wrote, *For it pleased the Father that in him should all fulness dwell.* Ephesians 1:20-23 expressed the same reality, *Which he wrought in Christ, when he raised him from the dead, and set him at his own right hand in the heavenly places, Far above all principality, and power, and might, and dominion, and every name that is named, not only in this world, but also in that which is to come: And hath put all things under his feet, and gave him to be the head over all things to the church, Which is his body, the fulness of him that filleth all in all,* as does I Corinthians 15:23-28, *But every man in his own order: Christ the firstfruits; afterward they that are Christ's at his coming. Then cometh the end, when he shall have delivered up the kingdom to God, even the Father; when he shall have put down all rule and all authority and power. For he must reign, till he hath put all enemies under his feet. The last enemy that shall be destroyed is death. For he hath put all things under his feet. But when he saith all things are put under him, it is manifest that he is excepted, which did put all things under him. And when all things shall be subdued unto him, then shall the Son also himself be subject unto him* *that put all things under him, that God may be all in all.* Jesus is not just the path to life; He is life itself. He is not just the way to God; He is God Himself. Jesus is not just a good teacher; He is truth itself. Jesus is not just a prophet; He is the essence of history itself. He is not just a means by which we can be saved; He is salvation itself. He is all; without Him there is <u>absolutely</u> <u>nothing</u>!

No good storyteller gives away his punch line until the climax of the story, but I think that it might be worthwhile to violate that principle just this once and tell you that the punch line of the book comes in verse 1:27 when Paul speaks of the *riches of the glory of this mystery among the Gentiles which is Christ in you, the hope of glory.* The point of his whole epistle is that this incomprehensible Christ – the Creator, the Head of the Church, the Redeemer, the Image of God, the Sustainer, the Totality of everything – actually lives inside us!! How phenomenal!! How powerful!! How victoriously liberating!!

> *But the righteousness which is of faith speaketh on this wise, Say not in thine heart, Who shall ascend into heaven? (that is, to bring Christ down from above:) Or, Who shall descend into the deep? (that is, to bring up Christ again from the dead.) But what saith it? The word is nigh thee, even in thy mouth, and in thy heart: that is, the word of faith, which we preach; That if thou shalt confess with thy mouth the Lord Jesus, and shalt believe in thine heart that God hath raised him from the dead, thou shalt be saved. For with the heart man believeth unto righteousness; and with the mouth confession is made unto salvation.* (Romans 10:6-10)

Through the first word, we were able to learn what Colossians has to say about who Christ is. In the second word, we will discover what it is that He has given us. This theme is based on the reference in Colossians 1:13 where Paul says that we have been delivered from the power of darkness and are now translated into the kingdom of God's dear Son. Let's explore what exactly comprises this kingdom in which we now have citizenship by looking at the letters that spell "kingdom."

K stands for **K**nowledge, our key to the Divine Nature. Twice, Paul addresses the believers concerning the significance of the knowledge that we have received – or at least, should have received – concerning our new life in Christ. First he stresses its importance through the fact that it is an earnest prayer on his part that they be awakened to this life-changing knowledge, *For this cause we also, since the day we heard it, do not cease to pray for you, and to desire that ye might be filled with the knowledge of his will in all wisdom and spiritual understanding; That ye might walk worthy of the Lord unto all pleasing, being fruitful in every good work, and increasing in the knowledge of God.* (verses 1:9-10) As the apostle Peter would tell us, we are stewards of the manifold grace of God. (I Peter 4:10) Next, Paul confides in them that he feels that the treasures they will obtain through this knowledge are worth the great conflict he has to endure in order to get them to receive the revelation, *For I would that ye knew what great conflict I have for you, and for them at Laodicea, and for as many as have not seen my face in the flesh; That their hearts might be comforted, being knit together in love, and unto all riches of the full assurance of understanding, to the acknowledgement of the mystery of God, and of the Father, and of Christ; In whom are hid all the treasures of wisdom and knowledge.* (verses 2:1-3) In verse 4:5, he makes one additional reference to wisdom, the by-product of properly applied knowledge when he admonishes them to walk in wisdom toward them that are without, redeeming the time – in other words, he wants them to live their lives before unbelievers in light of the knowledge they have received when they were translated out of the kingdom under which they lived their lives and into the new kingdom under whose rule we now live. In his parallel book of Ephesians, Paul makes essentially identical statements, in what I consider to be the greatest apostolic prayer recorded in the scripture, concerning the significance of this knowledge, [I]

Cease not to give thanks for you, making mention of you in my prayers; That the God of our Lord Jesus Christ, the Father of glory, may give unto you the spirit of wisdom and revelation in the knowledge of him: The eyes of your understanding being enlightened; that ye may know what is the hope of his calling, and what the riches of the glory of his inheritance in the saints. (verses 1:16-18) However, it is the Apostle Peter who gives us a really clear comprehension of the power of this knowledge, *Grace and peace be multiplied unto you through the knowledge of God, and of Jesus our Lord, According as his divine power hath given unto us all things that pertain unto life and godliness, through the knowledge of him that hath called us to glory and virtue: Whereby are given unto us exceeding great and precious promises: that by these ye might be partakers of the divine nature, having escaped the corruption that is in the world through lust.* (II Peter 1:2-4) Notice all the benefits that come to us when we comprehend and apply this knowledge: grace, peace, all things that pertain to life and godliness, exceeding great and precious promises, and the divine nature. Before we go too far in considering this passage, I want to point out something that is hidden in the Greek text of this verse. The words for "knowledge" and "lust" both bear the prefix *epi* that means "all-encompassing." In other words, the apostle is not talking about just a casual knowledge or desire, but a full-throttle revelation and a raging craving. The all-encompassing knowledge of God means that we will see every aspect of our lives from God's perspective. In business, we will see God's hand in the way we make transactions; in the home, we will see God at work in every relationship; in planning our future, we will see God guiding in each step; in everything, we will see God as ever-present. On the flipside of the coin, there is an all-encompassing lust, a me-centered attitude that is always looking for what I can get out of every deal and relationship. This me-centered lust goes far beyond sexual attractions that we customarily associate with the term; it reaches into the arenas of finance, power, position, and prestige – every aspect of life. Peter concludes that a life lived under its domination will be characterized by corruption like a putrid, running sore. The life characterized by the all-encompassing knowledge of God culminates in the divine nature – we actually take on the character and qualities of God Himself!! Romans 12: 2 says that we actually have the capability of not conforming to this world but being transformed by the renewing of our minds through this knowledge of God. The result is that we will prove (or live out) the good, acceptable, and perfect will of God in our lives!

I represents our **I**nheritance, our invitation to the Divine Promises. *Giving thanks unto the Father, which hath made us meet to be partakers of the inheritance of the saints in light.* (verse 1:12) *Knowing that of the Lord ye shall receive the reward of the inheritance: for ye serve the Lord Christ.* (verse 3:24) When speaking of the inheritance we have awaiting us, it would be good to back up a bit and remember that we have been made heirs to these promises and provisions due to having been adopted into the family of God. The practice of adoption in biblical times was for providing an avenue of passing on an inheritance. If a man had no son, he would usually adopt a nephew to become his heir. This practice kept the wealth inside the family, rather than letting it be lost to outsiders. Notice in the story of Abraham and Lot that it was only after Lot had separated from Abraham (Genesis 13:14) that Abraham became concerned about the fact that he had no heir (Genesis 15:2). Unlike adoption today, which may be based on sympathy for orphaned children or the loneliness of childless couples, biblical adoption was based solely on the desire to pass on benefits. If we see our position in Christ in this light, we will understand that God <u>wants</u> to make an investment in us. We don't have to beg or coerce Him into blessing us. He went out of His way to make His blessing available to us. Andrew Wommack likens our pursuing after the blessing that God has already given us to a dog chasing its tail – he's trying to get something that he already has. Passages from Ephesians parallel and enhance the ideas we find in Colossians. *In whom also we have obtained an inheritance, being predestinated according to the purpose of him who worketh all things after the counsel of his own will.* (verse 1:11) *Which is the earnest of our inheritance until the redemption of the purchased* *possession, unto the praise of his glory.* (verse 1:14) *The eyes of your understanding being enlightened; that ye may know what is the hope of his calling, and what the riches of the glory of his inheritance in the saints.* (verse 1:18) *For this ye know, that no whoremonger, nor unclean person, nor covetous man, who is an idolater, hath any inheritance in the kingdom of Christ and of God.* (verse 5:5) God has prepared an inheritance for us and He is actually more eager to get it to us than we might be about receiving it. Deuteronomy 28:2 says that the blessings of God are pursuing us and chasing us down. Maybe some of us need to slow down a bit and let them catch up.

N is for our **New** Identity, our translation to a Divine Position. Although I have already quoted verse 1:13, we need to look at it again because of its significance at this point, *Who hath delivered us from the power of darkness, and hath translated us into the kingdom of his dear Son.* Before we accepted Jesus, we were subjects of the kingdom of darkness, having an identity with the carnal, natural – even diabolical and demonic – realm. Once we accepted Christ into our lives, we passed from death unto life (I John 3:14) and took on the identity of the spirit – even the divine nature. The classic description of this transformation is found in II Corinthians 5:17, *Therefore if any man be in Christ, he is a new creature: old things are passed away; behold, all things are become new.* It might be beneficial to go back to the Garden of Eden to see the dramatic change that originally occurred when man first became subject to the kingdom of darkness; in doing so, we will get a glimpse of how significant a change we should expect when leaving that kingdom to re-enter the kingdom of light. Prior to their disobedience, Adam and Eve lived in splendid harmony with God. They were loyal subjects of His kingdom; and, as such, they were not even mildly influenced by the flesh or the law of sin and death. A clear demonstration of this freedom is seen in Genesis 2:25 that says that they were naked and not ashamed. They were so spiritually minded that they didn't even notice the nakedness of their flesh. However, all that changed instantly with the first taste of the forbidden fruit. Genesis 3:7 records that they instantly saw that they were naked and started trying to fashion clothes from fig leaves. Furthermore, this carnal orientation was not just an addition to their spiritual side; carnality actually became a replacement for spirituality, demonstrated by their unwillingness to meet with God because of their nakedness. (verse 3:10) Their obsession with their flesh had routed out their fellowship with God. Now that we have been offered the possibility of being translated into the kingdom of God's dear son, we have the opportunity to reverse this situation and become spiritually minded rather than carnally minded. (Romans 8:6) I'm not advocating nudity but a mental change that is so radical that our focus changes as dramatically as did that of our first father and mother – only our new mentality is now back on the positive, spiritual side of life and off of the negative, carnal side. When Paul wrote to the Ephesians about this new identity, he went a step further than just being invited to walk with God as Adam and Eve did; he added the dimension of having been actually invited to sit with Him in His dominion. "And hath raised us up together, and made us sit together in heavenly places in Christ Jesus." (Ephesians 2:6) *Which he wrought in Christ, when he raised him from the dead, and set him at his own right hand in the heavenly places, Far above all principality, and power, and might, and dominion, and every name that is named, not only in this world, but also in that which is to come.* (Ephesians 1:20-21) We are invited into this new kingdom, not only as citizens who are privileged to have fellowship with the King, but also as ones who are bidden to share with Him in His kingdom's authority.

G reminds us of **Grace** that is our blessing of Divine Favor. Paul writes to the Colossians not only about their experiencing grace, but also showing grace to others. *To the saints and faithful brethren in Christ which are at Colosse: Grace be unto you, and peace, from God our Father and the Lord Jesus Christ.* (verse 1:2) *Which is come unto you, as it is in all the world; and bringeth forth fruit, as it doth also in you, since the day ye heard of it, and knew the grace of God in truth.* (verse 1:6) *Let the word of Christ dwell in you richly in all wisdom; teaching and admonishing one another in psalms* *and hymns and spiritual songs, singing with grace in your hearts to the Lord.* (verse 3:16) *Let your speech be alway with grace, seasoned with salt, that ye may know how ye ought to answer every man.* (verse 4:6)

Someone once defined grace as "God's resources at Christ's expense." This seems to be a fairly accurate description in that it makes us aware that our forgiveness and acceptance are not merited by our own good deeds or altruistic works but by the unmerited favor of God toward us that was purchased on Calvary. (Ephesians 2:8) When we show grace to others, again it is not our own meritorious deeds or altruism at work but the unmerited favor of God manifesting through us. In the companion volume of Ephesians, Paul speaks of grace at least ten times (Ephesians 1:6, 7; 2:5, 7, 8; 3:2, 7, 8; 4:7, 29); however, I want to focus on only one specific phrase. In verse 1:7-8, Paul speaks of *riches of his grace wherein he hath abounded toward us.* In chapter two verse seven, he amplifies his description of grace to speak of the *exceeding riches of his grace in his kindness toward us through Christ Jesus.* Ephesians 1:7-8 in the New International Version reads, *In him we have redemption through his blood, the forgiveness of sins, in accordance with the riches of God's grace that he lavished on us with all wisdom and understanding.* To understand what the word "lavished" means, I need to give another little illustration. I stopped by a fast food restaurant one day and ordered a sandwich. I watched as the little girl with a plastic glove reached into a bin of meat and took out a handful. She then dropped it onto a scale and began to pick off little pieces of meat to make sure that I was not going to get more than four ounces. Becoming a bit offended as I watched her meticulously guard the company's profits, I made a decision that my next meal would be across the street at the all-you-can-eat steak house where I could choose from salads, hot entrees, grilled-to-order steaks, and desserts and I could eat until I could barely waddle out. My son once ate twelve steaks at this place for essentially the same price I paid for my four ounces of shaved roast beef! When it comes to understanding the grace of God, we need to realize that He is like the smorgasbord – He spreads a lavish table before us, more than we could ever use and even more than we could ever think to ask for! (Ephesians 3:20)

The letter **D** is to remind us to **D**emonstrate the Fruit of the Spirit, our manifestation of Divine Life. It is interesting that all of the nine manifestations of the fruit of the spirit as listed in Galatians chapter five are addressed in this tiny book of Colossians.

Love: *Since we heard of your faith in Christ Jesus, and of the love which ye have to all the saints.* (verse 1:4) *Who also declared unto us your love in the Spirit.* (verse 1:8) *That their hearts might be comforted, being knit together in love, and unto all riches of the full assurance of understanding, to the acknowledgement of the mystery of God, and of the Father, and of Christ.* (verse 2:2) *Husbands, love your wives, and be not bitter against them.* (verse 3:19)

Joy: *Strengthened with all might, according to his glorious power, unto all patience and longsuffering with joyfulness.* (verse 1:11)

Peace: *To the saints and faithful brethren in Christ which are at Colosse: Grace be unto you, and peace, from God our Father and the Lord Jesus Christ.* (verse 1:2) *And, having made peace through the blood of his cross, by him to reconcile all things unto himself; by him, I say, whether they be things in earth, or things in heaven.* (verse 1:20) *And let the peace of God rule in your hearts, to the which also ye are called in one body; and be ye thankful.* (verse 3:15)

Longsuffering: *Strengthened with all might, according to his glorious power, unto all patience and longsuffering with joyfulness.* (verse 1:11) *Put on therefore, as the elect of God, holy and beloved, bowels of mercies, kindness, humbleness of mind, meekness, longsuffering.* (verse 3:12)

Gentleness: *Let the word of Christ dwell in you richly in all wisdom; teaching and admonishing one another in psalms and hymns and spiritual songs, singing with grace in your hearts to the Lord.* (verse 3:16) *Let your speech be alway with grace, seasoned with salt, that ye may know how ye ought to answer every man.* (verse 4:6)

Goodness: *That ye might walk worthy of the Lord unto all pleasing, being fruitful in every good work, and increasing in the knowledge of God.* (verse 1:10)

Faith: *Since we heard of your faith in Christ Jesus, and of the love which ye have to all the saints.* (verse 1:4) *If ye continue in the faith grounded and settled, and be not moved away from the hope of the gospel, which ye have heard, and which was preached to every creature which is under heaven; whereof I Paul am made a minister.* (verse 1:23) *For though I be absent in the flesh, yet am I with you in the spirit, joying and beholding your order, and the stedfastness of your faith in Christ.* (verse 2:5) *Rooted and built up in him, and stablished in the faith, as ye have been taught, abounding therein with thanksgiving.* (verse 2:7) *Buried with him in baptism, wherein also ye are risen with him through the faith of the operation of God, who hath raised him from the dead.* (verse 2:12)

Meekness: *Put on therefore, as the elect of God, holy and beloved, bowels of mercies, kindness, humbleness of mind, meekness, longsuffering.* (verse 3:12)

Temperance: *Mortify therefore your members which are upon the earth; fornication, uncleanness, inordinate affection, evil concupiscence, and covetousness, which is idolatry.* (verse 3:5)

O represents the **O**vercoming Power that is our guarantee of Divine Victory. Notice the emphasis Paul places on the power of God that is at work in us. He says that we are *strengthened with all might, according to his glorious power* (verse 1:11) and that the efforts he put forth in the gospel were actually the strivings of God working through him mightily (verse 1:29). He recognizes that it is not his or our ability, but the mighty ability of God working through him and us that makes a difference. Verse fifteen of chapter two is the climax of the discussion on this powerful authority, *And having spoiled principalities and powers, he made a shew of them openly, triumphing over them in it.* The historical context of the imagery used in this passage comes from the ancient practice of humiliating conquered enemies to show that they have been totally subjugated. The term "spoil" means "to strip naked," a reference to the practice of stripping away every vestige of position, authority, honor, and respect from a defeated foe. No longer would the king have his crown, the general his stripes, the athlete his accolades, the soldier his medals, the judge his regalia, the scholar his mortarboard, or the priest his rosary. Now, naked as the day they were born, they would be marched through the streets for all to see that these once feared and respected individuals have nothing to trust in or boast of. Paul furthers this imagery in his second epistle to the Corinthians. In chapter two verse fourteen, he says that God always causes us to triumph in Christ, and in chapter ten verses four and five, he speaks of the weapons of our warfare that are mighty through God to pull down strongholds, to cast down imaginations and every high thing that exalts itself against the knowledge of God, and to bring every thought into captivity to the obedience of Christ. The mention of "triumph" is a reference to the Roman practice of marching defeated enemies and all the confiscated treasures through the arch of triumph in celebration of the victory. In this parade, the enemies who were formerly threats are now displayed as slaves with no power or authority. Paul says that God is working in us to bring the enemy of our souls, the devil, to this public display of humiliation in our lives.

The key word "kingdom" concludes with the letter **M** signifying **M**ystery, our participation in the Divine Plan. In verses twenty-six and twenty-seven of the first chapter, Paul says, *Even the mystery which hath been hid from ages and from generations, but now is made manifest to his saints: To whom God would make known what is the riches of the glory of this mystery among the Gentiles; which is Christ in you, the hope of glory.* He also mentions this mystery in chapter two verse two,

That their hearts might be comforted, being knit together in love, and unto all riches of the full assurance of understanding, to the acknowledgement of the mystery of God, and of the Father, and of Christ, and chapter four verse three, *Withal praying also for us, that God would open unto us a door of utterance, to speak the mystery of Christ.* We have already mentioned that the fact that "Christ in us" is the punch line of the letter. The full message of this epistle is that the very Christ of God is not just on His exalted throne far above but right inside of us, a second throne from which He can exercise His majestic authority! This revelation is a mystery in the same sense as the punch line of any story has to be kept "under wraps" until just the right time for it to have its full effect. The unfortunate thing about this mystery is that all too many of us who actually have Christ inside of us haven't yet caught on. We are still living as if Christ is somewhere far removed from us and that we still have to fight our battles in our own strength. It is time we catch on to the punch line and put a lot more "punch" into life by letting the Christ of the universe rule from inside our personal universes! In Galatians 2:20, Paul made an excellent distillation of this reality when he wrote, *I am crucified with Christ: nevertheless I live; yet not I, but Christ liveth in me: and the life which I now live in the flesh I live by the faith of the Son of God, who loved me, and gave himself for me.* This was his personal revelation of the mystery – his hope of glory!

One of the most significant (in reality, every word of this epistle is significant) passages in the little book is Colossians 3:1, *If ye then be risen with Christ, seek those things which are above, where Christ sitteth on the right hand of God.* A second verse of parallel significance is Colossians 2:12, *Buried with him in baptism, wherein also ye are risen with him through the faith of the operation of God, who hath raised him from the dead.* These two verses speak of the fact that we have been raised up by Christ and then go on to show us that we must live different lives as a result of what Christ has done in us. Because we have been changed, we should show forth some real changes. Let's look at the word "raised" in order to see how we are expected to respond to the change that Christ has made in us.

R represents our obligation to **R**eceive Him, allowing Christ to Enter into us. *Knowing that of the Lord ye shall receive the reward of the inheritance: for ye serve the Lord Christ. But he that doeth wrong shall receive for the wrong which he hath done: and there is no respect of persons.* (verses 3:24-25) *And you, that were sometime alienated and enemies in your mind by wicked works, yet now hath he reconciled."* (verse 1:21) In the book of Revelation, John expresses the heart of the Lord who has been locked out of the hearts and lives of men, *Behold, I stand at the door, and knock: if any man hear my voice, and open the door, I will come in to him, and will sup with him, and he with me.* (verse 3:20) Once we were alienated from God and were without an inheritance, but our simple act of opening our heart's door to Christ is all that is required for us to come into this radically new relationship that Paul is describing in this letter.

A stands for **A**dvance, allowing Christ to Motivate us. Paul makes the point several times that we must not stand still, or stagnate, in our experience with Christ. Instead, we are to make positive, forward steps to walk out our faith and experience. *That ye might walk worthy of the Lord unto all pleasing, being fruitful in every good work, and increasing in the knowledge of God.* (verse 1:10) *As ye have therefore received Christ Jesus the Lord, so walk ye in him.* (verse 2:6) *Walk in wisdom toward them that are without, redeeming the time.* (verse 4:5)

In Galatians 5:25, the Apostle Paul admonished us, *If we live in the Spirit, let us also walk in the Spirit.* There is a tremendous difference between living and walking. Our being alive is dependent on others, but walking is self-dependent. It is our mother and father who are responsible for our being alive, but we are individually responsible for our walking. Any time we let someone else do our walking, we cease to walk and start to ride. In the spiritual realm, we are alive because of

God's action, *For God so loved the world, that he gave his only begotten Son, that whosoever believeth in him should not perish, but have everlasting life.* (John 3:16) *And so it is written, The first man Adam was made a living soul; the last Adam was made a quickening spirit.* (I Corinthians 15:45) Yet, God allows us to do our own spiritual walking. He will guide our steps and support us if we falter, but He will not do our walking for us. One fast food restaurant boasts, "We do it all for you." But God doesn't make that same claim. He will give us dramatic instant deliverances, but then He commands us to follow through with the day-to-day disciplined walk that lives out that deliverance.

Walking has to do with progression. Unlike plants that are stationary, man can advance and move forward. In Japan, I saw a Bonsai tree the size of a seedling although it was seventy-five years old. In the mountains of California, I once viewed the Bristol Pines that are almost four thousand years old but about the size of regular trees. A few miles away, I marveled at the giant sequoia trees and redwoods that are almost as old but massive enough to prove their age. Regardless of how long these trees had lived, none of them had moved even an inch away from where they first sprouted. They had life, but not progress. Man, on the other hand, has the potential to progress; he can move forward; he can achieve; he does not have to remain stationary and stagnant. If a man does not progress, he is considered to be "vegetating" – becoming like one of those stuck-in-the-same-spot trees. Perhaps this is why the Bible speaks so frequently and pointedly about walking. God wants us to be progressive achievers.

When Paul challenged the Roman believers to walk in newness of life (Romans 6:4), he seemed to have handpicked his terms. He chose the Greek word for "walk" that means to progress at one's own volition, rather than the term that implies a regimented march. Thus, he suggests that the Christian walk is to proceed from the freshness of the spirit man, rather than from a mechanical following of the letter of the law. The term "newness" means new in nature rather than simply new in time. Three Greek words were available for the apostle to choose from for the word "life." His choice was *zoe* (the life of the spirit man), rather than *bios* (the life of the physical man), or *psyche* (the life of the soulical part of man). In other words, our Christian walk is not to be an emotionless march through life dictated by a disciplined system of "do"s and "don't"s barked out at us by a spiritual drill sergeant; rather, we are to be always progressing, but not on a regimented timetable that prohibits us from stopping to smell the roses along the way. Walking in the newness of life is walking in the spirit where there is liberty, righteousness, peace, and joy.

I comes next to remind us of the significance and necessity of Initiation Rituals that demonstrate that Christ is Transforming us. The apostle speaks of two different initiation rituals – circumcision, an Old Testament practice to demonstrate that the recipient is in covenant relationship with God, and baptism, the New Testament symbolism of identification with the death and resurrection of Christ. The first of these two rituals shows that we have been cut off from the old kingdom and made recipients of the blessings of the new kingdom. The second of these rituals signifies that we have died to the old sin-dominated life and been raised with the freedom to live a new sin-free life now that Christ has erased the rap sheet that Satan held against us. *In whom also ye are circumcised with the circumcision made without hands, in putting off the body of the sins of the flesh by the circumcision of Christ: Buried with him in baptism, wherein also ye are risen with him through the faith of the operation of God, who hath raised him from the dead. And you, being dead in your sins and the uncircumcision of your flesh, hath he quickened together with him, having forgiven you all trespasses; Blotting out the handwriting of ordinances that was against us, which was contrary to us, and took it out of the way, nailing it to his cross.* (verses 2:11-14)

In verses eight through thirteen of the third chapter, he furthers the discussion with some allusions that may not be

94

immediately understood in our modern culture. *But now ye also put off all these; anger, wrath, malice, blasphemy, filthy communication out of your mouth. Lie not one to another, seeing that ye have put off the old man with his deeds; And have put on the new man, which is renewed in knowledge after the image of him that created him: Where there is neither Greek nor Jew, circumcision nor uncircumcision, Barbarian, Scythian, bond nor free: but Christ is all, and in all. Put on therefore, as the elect of God, holy and beloved, bowels of mercies, kindness, humbleness of mind, meekness, longsuffering; Forbearing one another, and forgiving one another, if any man have a quarrel against any: even as Christ forgave you, so also do ye.* The first-century church practiced an additional step in their baptisms that has been lost somewhere along the way. When the candidate went down into the river for baptism, he would wear his old cloak that was certainly soiled from daily wear and possibly tattered and stained. As he came up from the waters of baptism, he would discard the old cloak for a beautiful new cloak that was spotlessly white. Paul admonishes his readers to follow through with the symbolism and apply it to their own lives by ridding themselves of motivations, actions, and habits that are spots ruining their spiritual garments while accepting the new spotless robe of Christ's righteousness.

The **S** brings us back to the fact that Christ has **S**poiled Principalities, the reality that Christ is Empowering us. Although we have previously discussed this point, it is worthy to be repeated here since it is a key to the whole book. *And having spoiled principalities and powers, he made a shew of them openly, triumphing over them in it.* (verse 2:15)

E is for **E**stablished, the fact that Christ secures us. Notice the powerful adjectives, "perfect" and "complete," used in the following passages: *Whom we preach, warning every man, and teaching every man in all wisdom; that we may present every man perfect in Christ Jesus.* (verses 1:28) *Epaphras, who is one of you, a servant of Christ, saluteth you, always labouring fervently for you in prayers, that ye may*

stand perfect and complete in all the will of God. (verse 4:12)
*And ye are complete in him, which is the head of all
principality and power.* (verse 2:10) If only we could really
grasp the reality and significance of these verses, we would
never again allow the "Christians aren't perfect, just forgiven"
bumper stickers on our cars or make apologies like, "Well, I'm
only human," or "Well, none of us are perfect." In reality, we
are perfect in God's eyes because His perfect Son lives in us!

      "Raised" concludes with a **D** signifying that we are to
Demonstrate our faith in Practical Ways, allowing Christ to
Manifest through us. Here, Paul gives us some where-the-
rubber-meets-the-road counsel on living the Christian life. He
writes, *And above all these things put on charity, which is the
bond of perfectness. And let the peace of God rule in your
hearts, to the which also ye are called in one body; and be ye
thankful. Let the word of Christ dwell in you richly in all
wisdom; teaching and admonishing one another in psalms and
hymns and spiritual songs, singing with grace in your hearts to
the Lord. And whatsoever ye do in word or deed, do all in the
name of the Lord Jesus, giving thanks to God and the Father
by him.* (verses 3:14-17) The following verses show how this
love will play out in our home and business relationships. He
then wraps up the discussion with the admonition, *Continue in
prayer, and watch in the same with thanksgiving; Withal
praying also for us, that God would open unto us a door of
utterance, to speak the mystery of Christ, for which I am also in
bonds: That I may make it manifest, as I ought to speak. Walk
in wisdom toward them that are without, redeeming the time.
Let your speech be alway with grace, seasoned with salt, that
ye may know how ye ought to answer every man.* (verses 4:2-6)
I find it significant how often he says "let." For Paul, the
Christian life isn't about what we are doing; it's all about
allowing the new life of Christ manifest itself through us.
      In this little epistle Paul twice refers to our being holy.
This concept might seem foreign to many modern-day
believers who look at their failure-ridden lives and wonder
what the Colossians might have had that they do not. The fact
that we are holy refers to our position in Christ more than what

we normally consider holiness to be – perfection. I'm sure that we've all heard the expression, "a face that only a mother could love." The imagery here is that the mother loves the baby or child and sees him as beautiful even though he is ugly in everyone's eyes. I remember one friend coming to me for counseling over a jealousy issue because he felt that all the men around were "hitting on" his beautiful wife. When I met the wife, I thought to myself, "This guy doesn't need counseling; he needs an eye exam." As rude and crude as these examples may be, they help to explain the point that when others – or even we ourselves – look at our lives, we probably wouldn't use the term "holy" to describe them. Jesus, on the other hand, can't help but see us as holy because He is looking through eyes of pure love. Again, we can get a better understanding of this truth by using the letters of the word as an acrostic to investigate the elements that comprise this truth.

H stands for **H**is viewpoint. It is God's perspective, not our own, that is important when we consider our relationship to Him. If we look at our mistakes, accidents, and even deliberate misdeeds, we will never feel that we are acceptable to God; Satan, the accuser (Revelation 12:10) will see to that. However, if we could only look at ourselves through God's eyes, we would see that the filter of Jesus' blood that has been applied to our lives filters out all these shortcomings. (I John 1:9) Notice that Paul's statement in chapter one verse twenty-two says that we are *holy and unblameable and unreproveable in his sight.* We may not necessarily be in such good standing in our own eyes; but it is His perspective that counts, not ours! Though one single reference in scripture would be sufficient to prove a point unquestionable, let's take just a minute to peruse the scriptures to confirm that God anticipates that His people be without fault and blameless. The scriptures teach that our perfection should not be just in the way God sees us, but that we should actually mature into our Christ life to the point that the lives that He sees as faultless also become manifest to the world. *To the end he may stablish your hearts unblameable in holiness before God, even our Father, at the coming of our Lord Jesus Christ with all his saints.* (I Thessalonians 3:13)

According as he hath chosen us in him before the foundation of the world, that we should be holy and without blame before him in love. (Ephesians 1:4) *Who shall also confirm you unto the end, that ye may be blameless in the day of our Lord Jesus Christ.* (I Corinthians 1:8) *That ye may be blameless and harmless, the sons of God, without rebuke, in the midst of a crooked and perverse nation, among whom ye shine as lights in the world.* (Philippians 2:15) *Concerning zeal, persecuting the church; touching the righteousness which is in the law, blameless.* (Philippians 3:6) *And the very God of peace sanctify you wholly; and I pray God your whole spirit and soul and body be preserved blameless unto the coming of our Lord Jesus Christ.* (I Thessalonians 5:23) *A bishop then must be blameless, the husband of one wife, vigilant, sober, of good behaviour, given to hospitality, apt to teach.* (I Timothy 3:2) *And let these also first be proved; then let them use the office of a deacon, being found blameless.* (I Timothy 3:10) *And these things give in charge, that they may be blameless.* (I Timothy 5:7) *If any be blameless, the husband of one wife, having faithful children not accused of riot or unruly.* (Titus 1:6) *For a bishop must be blameless, as the steward of God; not selfwilled, not soon angry, not given to wine, no striker, not given to filthy lucre.* (Titus 1:7) *Wherefore, beloved, seeing that ye look for such things, be diligent that ye may be found of him in peace, without spot, and blameless.* (II Peter 3:14) *Now unto him that is able to keep you from falling, and to present you faultless before the presence of his glory with exceeding joy.* (Jude 1:24) *How much more shall the blood of Christ, who through the eternal Spirit offered himself without spot to God, purge your conscience from dead works to serve the living God?* (Hebrews 9:14) *And in their mouth was found no guile: for they are without fault before the throne of God.* (Revelation 14:5)

O helps us to remember to always be **O**riented toward heaven. In chapter three, Paul instructs us to *set your affection on things above, not on things on the earth. For ye are dead, and your life is hid with Christ in God. When Christ, who is our life, shall appear, then shall ye also appear with him in* *glory.* (verses 2-4) This was the same principle that he lived his own life by as he testified in Philippians 3:13-14, *Brethren, I count not myself to have apprehended: but this one thing I do, forgetting those things which are behind, and reaching forth unto those things which are before, I press toward the mark for the prize of the high calling of God in Christ Jesus.* Paul was able to endure incredible hardships in life because he was so focused on the heaven he was going to that he hardly noticed the hell he was going through!

L is a reminder to be **L**oyal in our own homes. Paul knew that if your faith doesn't work in the microcosm of your own home, there is no hope of its ever working in the macrocosm of the world; therefore, he made a point to instruct both the Colossians and the Ephesians to carefully put their faith into practice at home. Essentially, he was trying to tell us that if we can't make our faith work in our own houses, we can't expect it to work in God's house.

> *Wives, submit yourselves unto your own husbands, as it is fit in the Lord. Husbands, love your wives, and be not bitter against them. Children, obey your parents in all things: for this is well pleasing unto the Lord. Fathers, provoke not your children to anger, lest they be discouraged.* (verses 3:18-21)
> *Submitting yourselves one to another in the fear of God. Wives, submit yourselves unto your own husbands, as unto the Lord. For the husband is the head of the wife, even as Christ is the head of the church: and he is the saviour of the body. Therefore as the church is subject unto Christ, so let the wives be to their own husbands in every thing. Husbands, love your wives, even as Christ also loved the church, and gave himself for it; That he might sanctify and cleanse it with the washing of water by the word, That he*

might present it to himself a glorious church, not having spot, or wrinkle, or any such thing; but that it should be holy and without blemish. So ought men to love their wives as their own bodies. He that loveth his wife loveth himself. For no man ever yet hated his own flesh; but nourisheth and cherisheth it, even as the Lord the church: For we are members of his body, of his flesh, and of his bones. For this cause shall a man leave his father and mother, and shall be joined unto his wife, and they two shall be one flesh. This is a great mystery: but I speak concerning Christ and the church. Nevertheless let every one of you in particular so love his wife even as himself; and the wife see that she reverence her husband. Children, obey your parents in the Lord: for this is right. Honour thy father and mother; which is the first commandment with promise; That it may be well with thee, and thou mayest live long on the earth. And, ye fathers, provoke not your children to wrath: but bring them up in the nurture and admonition of the Lord. (Ephesians 5:21-6:4)

Rounding out the word is a **Y** representing **Y**ielding to Authority. In both Colossians and Ephesians, Paul instructs employees to submit to their employers as if working directly for God and for employers to treat their employees fairly, remembering that they too are employed by the Lord.

Servants, obey in all things your masters according to the flesh; not with eyeservice, as menpleasers; but in singleness of heart, fearing God: And whatsoever ye do, do it heartily, as to the Lord, and not unto men; Knowing that of the Lord ye shall receive the reward of the inheritance: for ye serve the

Lord Christ. But he that doeth wrong shall receive for the wrong which he hath done: and there is no respect of persons. Masters, give unto your servants that which is just and equal; knowing that ye also have a Master in heaven. (verses 3:22-4:1)
Servants, be obedient to them that are your masters according to the flesh, with fear and trembling, in singleness of your heart, as unto Christ; Not with eyeservice, as menpleasers; but as the servants of Christ, doing the will of God from the heart; With good will doing service, as to the Lord, and not to men: Knowing that whatsoever good thing any man doeth, the same shall he receive of the Lord, whether he be bond or free. And, ye masters, do the same things unto them, forbearing threatening: knowing that your Master also is in heaven; neither is there respect of persons with him. (Ephesians 6:5-9)

We might question why exactly we are to give heed to the authoritative teaching of Paul. What right does he have to speak so boldly into our lives? Paul couches his teachings on the one simple statement that he is an apostle. But what exactly does it mean to be an apostle and what weight does apostleship carry? Again, let's use the word as an acrostic to explore what clues we can find in the book of Colossians and Paul's other writings.

The **A** tells us that he was **A**ppointed to this mission. Twice, he assures us that he is not acting of his own will and volition, but under direct mandate of God. *Paul, an apostle of Jesus Christ by the will of God, and Timotheus our brother.* (verse 1:1) *Whereof I am made a minister, according to the dispensation of God which is given to me for you, to fulfil the word of God.* (verse 1:25) Similar affirmations are given at the opening of all his letters, including the companion volume,

Ephesians. *Paul, an apostle of Jesus Christ by the will of God, to the saints which are at Ephesus, and to the faithful in Christ Jesus.* (verse 1:1) In I Timothy 2:7, he goes a bit further and expands his job description to include a couple other hats, *Whereunto I am ordained a preacher, and an apostle, (I speak the truth in Christ, and lie not;) a teacher of the Gentiles in faith and verity.* His insistence that his mission was not of his own choosing but one thrust upon him by God is reminiscent of the words of Jesus in John 15:16, *Ye have not chosen me, but I have chosen you, and ordained you, that ye should go and bring forth fruit, and that your fruit should remain: that whatsoever ye shall ask of the Father in my name, he may give it you.*

When a person has a God-given ministry and appointment, that calling is not negotiable. In my own case, I have the calling and ministry of a teacher. In addition, I have other gifts that I can use to serve the Body of Christ, and on occasion I have been asked to serve in ministries where I could have functioned efficiently because of my gifts. However, taking these positions would have interfered with my calling, so I declined the offers. Once I was asked to pastor a church, but I explained to the denominational superintendent that my calling was to teach rather than to pastor. Amazingly, this high-ranking church leader didn't even understand the difference between the two ministries. Paul knew his calling, appointment, and ministry – and was dedicated to fulfilling it. We must also have that same clarity and commitment.

The **P** reminds me of one of the significant attributes that makes any leader worthy to speak into the lives of those under him – that he is a **P**rayer Warrior who genuinely holds them up in prayer before the throne of God. *We give thanks to God and the Father of our Lord Jesus Christ, praying always for you.* (verse 1:3) *For the hope which is laid up for you in heaven, whereof ye heard before in the word of the truth of the gospel.* (verse 1:5) *For this cause we also, since the day we heard it, do not cease to pray for you, and to desire that ye might be filled with the knowledge of his will in all wisdom and* *spiritual understanding.* (verse 1:9) Each of his letters opens with the same reassurance that he is baptizing his followers in prayer continually; however, the letter to the Ephesians contains the content of some of his prayers which give practical demonstration of how he interceded for them.

> *For this cause I bow my knees unto the Father of our Lord Jesus Christ, Of whom the whole family in heaven and earth is named, That he would grant you, according to the riches of his glory, to be strengthened with might by his Spirit in the inner man; That Christ may dwell in your hearts by faith; that ye, being rooted and grounded in love, May be able to comprehend with all saints what is the breadth, and length, and depth, and height; And to know the love of Christ, which passeth knowledge, that ye might be filled with all the fulness of God. Now unto him that is able to do exceeding abundantly above all that we ask or think, according to the power that worketh in us.* (verses 3:14-20)
>
> *Wherefore I also, after I heard of your faith in the Lord Jesus, and love unto all the saints, Cease not to give thanks for you, making mention of you in my prayers; That the God of our Lord Jesus Christ, the Father of glory, may give unto you the spirit of wisdom and revelation in the knowledge of him: The eyes of your understanding being enlightened; that ye may know what is the hope of his calling, and what the riches of the glory of his inheritance in the saints, And what is the exceeding greatness of his power to us-ward who believe, according to the working of his mighty power, Which he wrought in Christ, when he raised him from the dead, and set him at his own right hand*

in the heavenly places, Far above all principality, and power, and might, and dominion, and every name that is named, not only in this world, but also in that which is to come: And hath put all things under his feet, and gave him to be the head over all things to the church, Which is his body, the fulness of him that filleth all in all. (verses 1:15-23)

O stands for another qualification that is often lacking in the lives of leaders and would-be spokesmen of God – **O**ffering oneself for the followers. *Who now rejoice in my sufferings for you, and fill up that which is behind of the afflictions of Christ in my flesh for his body's sake, which is the church.* (verse 1:24) *For I would that ye knew what great conflict I have for you, and for them at Laodicea, and for as many as have not seen my face in the flesh.* (verse 2:1)

In II Corinthians 11:23-28, Paul describes all the tortures he experienced as a messenger of the Lord but concludes the section with the statement that the internal spiritual burden he bore for the churches was greater than the external physical weight he carried. *Are they ministers of Christ? (I speak as a fool) I am more; in labours more abundant, in stripes above measure, in prisons more frequent, in deaths oft. Of the Jews five times received I forty stripes save one. Thrice was I beaten with rods, once was I stoned, thrice I suffered shipwreck, a night and a day I have been in the deep; In journeyings often, in perils of waters, in perils of robbers, in perils by mine own countrymen, in perils by the heathen, in perils in the city, in perils in the wilderness, in perils in the sea, in perils among false brethren; In weariness and painfulness, in watchings often, in hunger and thirst, in fastings often, in cold and nakedness. Beside those things that are without, that which cometh upon me daily, the care of all the churches.* Later in the same book he declared that he would very gladly spend and be spent for their sake. (verse 12:15) However, it is in the book of Romans that he makes the ultimate expression of concern, saying that he would be willing to be accursed from Christ for his brethren if it would bring them to salvation. (verse 9:3) Truly, Paul had the heart of a leader that Jesus described as a true shepherd. (John 10:15) He was a true shepherd, not a hireling. (John 10:12-13)

S stands for Sharing, the quality of getting into the yoke with others and helping carry the burden and get the job done. Many church leaders today see themselves in positions of prominence rather than understanding that their calling is one of service. In Nigeria, I discovered that certain privileges (including even the brand of soft drink they were to drink) were reserved exclusively for bishops. In essence, they have set themselves apart from the general Christian population and even from other pastors. What a contrast from what we read in Paul's writings. In this letter, Paul mentions a number of individuals with whom he has become partners.

> *As ye also learned of Epaphras our dear fellowservant, who is for you a faithful minister of Christ.* (verse 1:7)
> *All my state shall Tychicus declare unto you, who is a beloved brother, and a faithful minister and fellowservant in the Lord: Whom I have sent unto you for the same purpose, that he might know your estate, and comfort your hearts; With Onesimus, a faithful and beloved brother, who is one of you. They shall make known unto you all things which are done here. Aristarchus my fellowprisoner saluteth you, and Marcus, sister's son to Barnabas, (touching whom ye received commandments: if he come unto you, receive him;) And Jesus, which is called Justus, who are of the circumcision. These only are my fellowworkers unto the kingdom of God, which have been a comfort unto me. For I bear him record, that he hath a great zeal for you, and them that are in Laodicea, and them in Hierapolis. Luke, the beloved*

physician, and Demas, greet you. Salute the brethren which are in Laodicea, and Nymphas, and the church which is in his house. And when this epistle is read among you, cause that it be read also in the church of the Laodiceans; and that ye likewise read the epistle from Laodicea. And say to Archippus, Take heed to the ministry which thou hast received in the Lord, that thou fulfil it. The salutation by the hand of me Paul. Remember my bonds. Grace be with you. Amen. (verses 4:7-18)

In II Corinthians 8:23, he speaks of Titus as his partner and fellow-helper. Timotheus was a close associate to Paul, who was listed as his workfellow in Romans 16:21, his brother, minister of God, and fellow-labourer in the gospel of Christ in I Thessalonians 3:2, and the only one likeminded who will naturally care for the state of the believers in Philippians 2:19-20. It is impossible to have a fellow-laborer unless you are also working. In other words, a true apostle doesn't mind rolling up his sleeves and getting his hands dirty with the work of the gospel.

The **T** draws our focus on **Truth**. *For the hope which is laid up for you in heaven, whereof ye heard before in the word of the truth of the gospel; Which is come unto you, as it is in all the world; and bringeth forth fruit, as it doth also in you, since the day ye heard of it, and knew the grace of God in truth.* (verses 1:5-6)

A genuine minister is one who tells the truth, the whole truth, and nothing but the truth, so help him God! Paul tells his followers on at least four occasions that he is telling them the truth and will not lie to them. (Romans 9:1, II Corinthians 11:31, Galatians 1:20, I Timothy 2:7) Something other than the truth or something less than the full truth may be more convenient, but in the long run will be harmful. A true minister knows that a half-truth is a full lie, and he will always lovingly speak the full truth. (Ephesians 4:15) He knows that the truth may hurt but that the lack of it will kill! The fact that ministry is founded on truth may seem to be so obvious that we would think that it need not even be discussed. It would be interesting to further this study in the three tiny books of First, Second, and Third John that have a combined total of only slightly over one hundred verses; yet, they contain over thirty references to the necessity of eliminating lies and turning to the truth.

The **L** in "apostle" is there to remind us of **L**ove, the foundation of all ministry. *Since we heard of your faith in Christ Jesus, and of the love which ye have to all the saints.* (verse 1:4) *Who also declared unto us your love in the Spirit.* (verse 1:8) *Who hath delivered us from the power of darkness, and hath translated us into the kingdom of his dear Son.* (verse 1:13) *That their hearts might be comforted, being knit together in love, and unto all riches of the full assurance of understanding, to the acknowledgement of the mystery of God, and of the Father, and of Christ.* (verse 2:2) *Husbands, love your wives, and be not bitter against them.* (verse 3:19) Though the entire New Testament is a treatise on the topic of love, we all know that First Corinthians chapter thirteen is the apex of the discussion for in that passage we learn that no ministry – no matter how spiritual it may seem, how dynamic it may appear, or how outstanding it may be – is worthwhile unless it is founded on and functioning through love. *Though I speak with the tongues of men and of angels, and have not charity, I am become as sounding brass, or a tinkling cymbal. And though I have the gift of prophecy, and understand all mysteries, and all knowledge; and though I have all faith, so that I could remove mountains, and have not charity, I am nothing. And though I bestow all my goods to feed the poor, and though I give my body to be burned, and have not charity, it profiteth me nothing.* (verses 1-3)

The word "apostle" ends with the letter **E**, appropriately symbolizing **E**ternity, the end focus of all ministry. True ministry will certainly help us deal with the issues of the here-and-now, but the ultimate goal is to prepare us for the return of the Lord and our eternal life with Him in heaven. *If ye then be risen with Christ, seek those things which are above, where Christ sitteth on the right hand of God. Set your affection on things above, not on things on the earth.* (verses 3:1-2) In Titus 2:13, Paul calls this eternal life our *blessed hope*, and in I Corinthians 15:19, he adds that if our only hope is in the present life *we are of all men most miserable.* John built on this truth to explain to us that every man who has this hope in him will purify himself and have a life that makes a difference in the here-and-now because of its focus on eternity. (I John 3:3)

We learned earlier that one of the key verses in Colossians is chapter two verse fifteen where Paul says that Christ has spoiled principalities and powers and made a public display of them as He triumphed over them. Before we conclude our study, it is appropriate that we re-visit this idea one last time – only this time we need to look at the flipside of the coin. Paul warned that it is also possible for our opponents to spoil believers, leaving them disarmed, disrobed, and humiliated just as Christ has done to the devil. In the word "spoil," we see five areas that we must guard to ensure our spiritual lives and the victories promised us in this letter.

The letter **S** stands for **S**eduction. When the enemy realizes that he can't take us down by force, he switches to a second approach. His plan B is to seduce us into believing his lies. Just as more women lose their virtue to men through seduction than to rape, it is more likely that Christians will be overcome by the enemy through his enticing lies than through outright onslaught. Paul warned the Colossians to be on guard *lest any man should beguile you with enticing words* (verse 2:4) and to *beware lest any man spoil you through philosophy and vain deceit, after the tradition of men, after the rudiments of the world, and not after Christ* (verse 2:8). In the companion letter to the Ephesians, the apostle gave two powerful keys for preventing such deception. In chapter four, he told them to submit themselves to the God-appointed leadership in the church so that they could mature to the point where they were no longer *children, tossed to and fro, and carried about with every wind of doctrine, by the sleight of men, and cunning craftiness, whereby they lie in wait to deceive.* (verses 11-14) In the following chapter, he instructed them to be followers of God, as dear children; and to walk in love, while avoiding fornication, all uncleanness, covetousness, filthiness, foolish talking, and jesting, guaranteeing that no one would deceive them with vain words. (verses 1-5)

P stands for **Pride**, which we all know is the precursor to destruction. (Proverbs 16:18) In the case of the Colossians, their weakness toward pride seemed to be camouflaged as humility – a false humility that actually boasts of how humble one is. It is possible to define pride as not how highly we think of ourselves but how often we think of ourselves. Unfortunately, in their quest to be humble, the Colossians had submitted themselves to spirits that demanded their obedience. As a result, they lost the freedom that Christ had purchased for them and they became subject to trying to merit their salvation. *Let no man beguile you of your reward in a voluntary humility and worshiping of angels, intruding into those things which he hath not seen, vainly puffed up by his fleshly mind.* (verse 2:18) Paul clearly explains that none of our good works are worthy of our pride. *Not of works, lest any man should boast.* (Ephesians 2:9) *Where is boasting then? It is excluded. By what law? of works? Nay: but by the law of faith* (Romans 3:27) He even goes so far in Philippians 3:4-8 to say,

> *Though I might also have confidence in the flesh. If any other man thinketh that he hath whereof he might trust in the flesh, I more: Circumcised the eighth day, of the stock of Israel, of the tribe of Benjamin, an Hebrew of the Hebrews; as touching the law, a Pharisee; Concerning zeal, persecuting the church; touching the righteousness which is in the law, blameless. But what things were gain to me, those I counted loss for Christ. Yea doubtless, and I count all things but loss*

*for the excellency of the knowledge of Christ
Jesus my Lord: for whom I have suffered the
loss of all things, and do count them but
dung, that I may win Christ.*

O represents **O**bligate, adding requirements to the grace of God. It has been said that Jesus plus nothing equals everything, but Jesus plus anything equals nothing. In other words, we negate salvation by grace alone through faith if we allow ourselves to be bound by any obligations other than simple trust in Christ. Paul warned the Colossians, *Let no man therefore judge you in meat, or in drink, or in respect of an holyday, or of the new moon, or of the sabbath days: Which are a shadow of things to come; but the body is of Christ.* (verses 2:16-17) When writing to the Galatians, Paul spoke extensively of this bondage (verses 2:4, 4:3, 4:9, 4:24, 4:25) and summed up the discussion in chapter five verse one by saying, *Stand fast therefore in the liberty wherewith Christ hath made us free, and be not entangled again with the yoke of bondage.*

I speaks of **I**gnoring the wonderful provisions that have been made available to us. He warns the Colossians not to let their relationship with Christ, the Head, slip. If they do so, he warns that they will forget that they are dead to the ordinances of this world and will fall again into trying to earn their salvation. *And not holding the Head, from which all the body by joints and bands having nourishment ministered, and knit together, increaseth with the increase of God. Wherefore if ye be dead with Christ from the rudiments of the world, why, as though living in the world, are ye subject to ordinances, (Touch not; taste not; handle not; Which all are to perish with the using;) after the commandments and doctrines of men? Which things have indeed a shew of wisdom in will worship, and humility, and neglecting of the body; not in any honour to the satisfying of the flesh.* (verses 2:19-23) The author of Hebrews gives us the bottom line on the topic in chapter two verse three when he writes, *How shall we escape, if we neglect so great salvation?*

The **L** that finishes out the word "spoil," represents the fact that we are **L**oosed from the things that once held us enslaved. *For which things' sake the wrath of God cometh on the children of disobedience: In the which ye also walked some time, when ye lived in them.* (verses 3:6-7) The parallel idea is presented in Paul's companion letter to the Ephesians, *Wherein in time past ye walked according to the course of this world, according to the prince of the power of the air, the spirit that now worketh in the children of disobedience...Let no man deceive you with vain words: for because of these things cometh the wrath of God upon the children of disobedience.* (verses 2:2, 5:6) *There is therefore now no condemnation to them which are in Christ Jesus, who walk not after the flesh, but after the Spirit.* (Romans 8:1)

The nineteenth-century Quaker author, Hannah Whitehall Smith wrote, "Dear friend, I make the glad announcement to thee that the Lord is in thy heart. Since the day of thy conversion He has been dwelling there, but thou hast lived on in ignorance of it. Every moment during all that time might have been passed in the sunshine of His sweet presence, and every step have been taken under His advice. But because thou knew it not, and did not look for Him there, thy life has been lonely and full of failure. But now that I make the announcement to thee, how wilt thou receive it? Art thou glad to have Him? Wilt thou consult Him about everything, and let Him into thy innermost chambers, and make Him the sharer in thy most hidden life? Wilt thou say 'Yes' to all His longing for union with thee, and with a glad and eager abandonment hand thyself and all that concerns thee over into His hands? If thou wilt, then shall thy soul begin to know something of the joy of union with Christ." If we do as Sister Smith has asked, we will have learned the colossal message of the book, that there is a mystery that has now been revealed – Christ living in us is our hope of glory. At that point, the message will become colossal within us!

Chapter Five
David Exposed

In 2004, Michelangelo's famous sculpture, <u>David</u>, went through an extensive cleaning and restoration process in celebration of its five-hundredth birthday. Half a millennium of grime has been removed to once again reveal the majestic splendor with which the masterpiece sparkled when it was first placed in the Piazza Signoria in Florence. This famous marble statue has often been noted as a most perfect depiction of the human body. And we often think of its subject – the biblical David – as being perfect as well. However, the wonderful thing about the Bible is that it tells the truth – even about its greatest heroes. They are presented to us as uncovered as Michelangelo's subject, with the only difference being that the Bible depicts its subjects with all their warts, mid-rib bulges, scars, and other defects. A careful reading of David's story, as God has had it preserved for us gives us, presents the picture of a man who was far from perfect. Actually, this is quite a relief for all of us imperfect humans – now we have a model of a man who, though as imperfect as we are, was still favored by God. Though David was as human as the rest of us, he maintained the testimony that he was a man after God's own heart. (Acts 13:22)

Though we want to be cautious not to err on the side of trying to be too honest and focusing too strongly on his defects, I think that we can benefit substantially by reviewing David's faults as well as his triumphs.

The one failure that comes to mind immediately when we think of King David is his moral failure with Bathsheba. The eleventh chapter of II Samuel records the story of how David spied her one evening as she bathed on the roof of the neighboring villa. Some students of the scripture and history have suggested that there might be more to the story than we notice on the first reading. They have suggested that this was not just her regular evening bath but was rather a special monthly ceremony she practiced to cleanse herself after her menstrual period. Assuming this to be the case, these scholars go on to surmise that David may have noticed this practice and even made a mental note of when to expect her next "performance." These students of the ancient culture then go on to suggest that David had actually planned to be there for the next "curtain call." They offer this as the explanation as to why David did not go out to battle with his men as was the custom of the kings (II Samuel 11:1) and the practice he followed until the very last days of his life when his men insisted that he remain behind for his own protection (II Samuel 21:17). Regardless as to whether this was a monthly or a nightly ritual with Bathsheba, the possibility remains that the fateful evening that has become a part of history was not the first time the king had noticed his neighbor's beauty. If this is the case, we see that the trap into which the king fell was one of his own making. Jesus taught us that looking upon a woman to lust after her is as great a sin as actually committing adultery with her. (Matthew 5:28) Notice that He didn't say "look upon a woman <u>and</u> lust after her," rather He said, *look upon a woman <u>to</u> lust after her*. The implication in His wording is that there is a difference between premeditated lust and instantaneous lustful thoughts that come when caught in a surprise situation. Did David know what he could expect to see when he looked over his portico that evening? Did he schedule his evening walk just so the timing would be right for the opening act? Did he stay home from the battle because he wanted to be in town for the next scheduled performance? If this is what happened, we see that the king was subject to a premeditated lust that destroyed him.

Yet, even if the lust was not something that the king had scheduled into his life, the episode exposes a serious flaw in David's moral fiber. An old saying tells us that we can't stop the birds from flying above our heads, but we can stop them from building a nest in our hair. Even if this was the first time he had ever noticed his voluptuous neighbor and this was the first time he had ever had wandering eyes, he was still guilty of not shooing away the birds of lustful thoughts before they had a chance to build a nest in his heart. James 1:14-15 tells us that sin is the result of temptation that is the product of lust. He adds that we are *drawn away by our own lust*, suggesting that lust is not an external temptation as much as it is an internal motivation. At first sighting of the maiden washing herself, he could have quickly turned away and gone back to bed; however, he chose rather to take a second glance, then a longer more intense look, then a stare, then a gaze before he returned to bed – unfortunately, he was not alone when he finally fell asleep again. David had followed the predictable pattern of allowing a temptation to take root inside his heart and develop into a lustful attitude that eventually resulted in acted out sin. David's most famous flaw was his moral failure with Bathsheba – the outgrowth of his lack of personal discipline over his thought life.

Immediately linked with his moral failure with Bathsheba was his gross failure in the arena of loyalty as demonstrated in his dealings with Uriah, Bathsheba's husband. Uriah, one of David's most able and dependable warriors, was away at battle at the time of the incident between his wife and the king. When David learned that Bathsheba was pregnant, he called her husband home from the front in order to make it appear that he was the father of the child. The scriptures record a remarkable story of Uriah's loyalty to the troops when he refused repeated offers to be with his wife, stating that he could not enjoy privileges that his men were being denied. What a picture of contrast between Uriah who refused his legitimate benefits in respect for his suffering troops and the king who indulged in not only his legitimate privileges but extended into illegitimate pleasures while his men suffered deprivation at the front. The end of the story is that David can think of no other solution than to have Uriah killed and marry Bathsheba with the hopes that no one would count to see if there were nine months between the royal wedding and the birth of the baby. In the most heinous deed of his career, David sent his loyal servant back to the front bearing his own death warrant.

115

An old song says that we only hurt the ones we love. I'm not sure if there is much validity to that analysis, but I'm certain that there is a lot of truth in the reverse of the saying: we seriously hurt the ones who love us. It is in betrayal of those who are loyal to us that we can inflict the deepest wounds. In David's dealing – or misdealings – with Uriah, we see one of his deepest flaws and most serious defects: his lack of loyalty.

Closely tied to his loyalty failure is David's failure with all his men. As we have already noticed, this episode in the life of David occurred at one point when he did not lead them into battle. These were the men whom he had taken when they were the misfits of society and had turned them into mighty warriors. They were ones whom he had personally transformed into heroes, yet this time their mentor was showing an example of a man who was more interested in his own personal leisure than their need for leadership. He had tragically failed them by abdicating his position of personal leadership before them at the front.

On top of all this, we see a failure against his position as king, his entire constituency, and himself in that he dishonestly tried to cover up the whole event. It was only when the prophet Nathan exposed the sin (II Samuel 12:7) that David was willing to admit and address his flaws.

Yet, his faults against Bathsheba, Uriah, and his troops were not nearly as serious as his failure toward God. David himself realized this when he framed his prayer recorded in Psalm fifty-one in which he repented for these atrocities. In verse four, David says, *Against You and You alone have I sinned*, indicating that he realized that the incidents involving adultery with Bathsheba, the murder of Uriah, and his disloyalty to the troops were only outward manifestations of the inward sin he had committed against God Himself. Apparently, David had slipped away from the intensity in his fellowship with and worship of God. He ends the psalm with a renewal in his commitment to worship, suggesting that he realized that his basic flaw was failing to pursue after the heart of God. When he spoke of his sin against God, David's word for "sin" can be interpreted with either meaning – "to miss the mark" or "to rebel." In essence, he had missed the mark by failing to intently follow after God's presence, resulting in a rebellion against His ways.

But David's failure toward God can also be seen as a failure toward himself. In another of the Psalms, he seems to have realized where he had gone wrong and requested divine protection to guard him against being trapped by the same pitfalls again. The Living Bible translation of Psalm 25:21 reads, *Assign me Godliness and Integrity as my bodyguards, for I expect you to protect me.* Having a bodyguard means the difference between life and death. When President Abraham Lincoln's bodyguard stepped out of the box in the Ford Theater, our sixteenth President was vulnerable and soon lay on the floor subject to John Wilkes Booth's bullet. President Ronald Reagan, on the other hand, survived an assassination attempt upon his life in 1981 when James Brady bravely threw his body as a human shield in front of John Hinckley Jr.'s bullet. When Godliness and Integrity were lacking, David was subject to the enemy's attacks.

The term "integrity" means "completeness." It implies a harmony or complete relationship with oneself. A person of integrity is one who is in harmony throughout his total personality. He doesn't think one thing and say another. He doesn't act one way and feel another. Integrity doesn't allow you to be dishonest or compromising. The term "godliness" may better be translated "uprightness," meaning equity. It means to be truthful and fair to all men. Godliness demands that you live like God in front of your fellowmen, not treat them like the devil. Integrity is being honest with yourself. Godliness is being honest with others. These two traits in David's lifestyle would have kept him safe from the assassination attempts of the world, the flesh, and the devil. In Psalm 119:11, he adds that the way he intends to ensure his protection against future sin is to hide the Word of God in his heart. Certainly, the engrafted Word of God produces integrity and uprightness.

In II Samuel chapter six, we read the enigmatic story of David's attempt to bring the Ark of the Covenant to Jerusalem. At first reading, it may seem that God unjustly took the life of Uzzah who tried to steady the Ark when it seemed to be tipping over as the oxcart jostled along the unpaved roadway. Yet, careful study of the passage will reveal that it was not a random, senseless act on God's part; rather, it was another of David's flaws that resulted in this innocent man's death. David had failed to understand the anointing of God. Just as Nadab and Abihu, the sons of Aaron, had been struck dead because they presented strange fire in the Tabernacle (Leviticus 10:1, Numbers 3:4, 26:61) and just as the two sons of Eli, Hophni and Phinehas, were slain because they desecrated the altar (I Samuel chapters one through four) and just as the Philistines had suffered severely when they held the Ark in their pagan temple and cities (I Samuel chapter five), David should have understood that he was endangering himself and anyone with him who would improperly approach God's sacred presence manifest in the Ark. Instead of taking precaution and showing holy reverence for the sacred object, David handled it much like any other piece of furniture, resulting in the tragic loss of a well-intentioned bystander. David's lack of recognition of and respect for the anointing of God certainly hurt him personally but, more seriously, hurt those for whom he was responsible.

Here again, we see that David's failure could have been avoided if only he had the Word of God hidden in his heart. Had he remembered Deuteronomy 10:8, he would have never placed the Ark on an oxcart as did the pagan Philistines but on the shoulders of the priests as did Moses. The surprising truth is that Deuteronomy 17:18 commanded that the kings of Israel handwrite their own personal copy of the Law. Had he been diligent to put it in his heart as he was committing it to paper, he would have diverted his own failure and the death of an innocent citizen.

Toward the end of his life, David demonstrated that he had a failure in the area of his faith life. This same king who had once penned the words of Psalm 20:7 declaring that he would not trust in military might but in the name of the Lord decided to take a census in order to determine the strength of his army. (II Samuel 24) This act of self-reliance rather than dependence upon the Lord made a major blotch on the record of his final days in office in that the judgment for this act brought a plague that took the lives of seventy thousand innocent civilians.

Possibly the greatest area of failure in David's life was in his failures as a parent. Though we do not know the stories – or even the names of most of David's offspring – the ones we do read about are full of tragedy and sadness. The baby born from the illegitimate relationship with Bathsheba died when only a few days old. Because of the immoral nature of the relationship between the parents, this unnamed soul was not covered by the divine blessing upon a covenant family. This child suffered because it was unconnected.

Tamar suffered because she was unprotected. Though her father knew all the details of the incestuous rape she had suffered in the tent of her half-brother, he did nothing to defend her honor or restore her dignity. Although David was very angry with Amnon, the young man who violated Tamar, the father never corrected the errant son for his crime. When Tamar's full-brother Absalom eventually took the life of the offender, he was punished by being estranged from his father; however, David never specifically addressed the need for correction for the homicide. In Amnon's case, David did nothing. Although he did measure out a form of punishment in the case of Absalom, he failed to correct him in the sense of imposing a punishment that would result in his rehabilitation. David failed these two sons in that they were uncorrected.

He failed two other sons in that they were left undirected. Although it was David's intention to establish Solomon as his successor, it seems that explicit directions to this effect were never given. The result was that Adonijah made an unsuccessful attempt to ascend to the throne when his father was no longer able to fulfill his royal duties. Bathsheba and the prophet Nathan who knew the king's intent rushed into the king's bedroom and informed him of Adonijah's move and motivated him to make a public announcement that Solomon was to succeed him as king. When I think of the scene of this bed-ridden monarch mustering enough energy to decree the next ruler of his nation, I realize how close this old man came to losing his chance to set things in order. Had he died before this announcement, a civil war could have been sparked. As it was, there was still unnecessary bloodshed and civil unrest that could have easily been avoided had he only taken time during his good years to direct his sons and present them with goals for their futures and strategies with which to accomplish these goals. David did use the closing days of his life to instruct his successor concerning his role as king; unfortunately, this should have been a lifelong lesson rather than a last-minute cram session. Perhaps it was because of the very conditions under which Solomon received his tutelage that he decided to do things differently for his son. He actually wrote him a manual on how to serve in his role as king – the book of Proverbs.

Though we have seen a number of flaws in David's character, we must graciously look beyond them to the positive qualities in this great leader. One outstanding area of David's life was his ability to establish and maintain godly relationships. His life illustrates how we should relate to the people with whom we live and work.

The first illustration has to do with the people who are above us. David had what could have been a major challenge in his life in dealing with the person above him: King Saul. Although David had done nothing to oppose the king, the young man became the target of the older man's violent hostilities. In addition to being an officer in the king's army and the king's personal musician, David was also the king's son-in-law and the closest friend of the king's son. In each of these relationships, Saul lashed out against his servant. As an officer, David found himself under the king's ire because the people celebrated his victories more than they did those of Saul. As the minstrel, he found himself the target of the king's javelin when the spirit enraged him. As the son-in-law and friend of the king's son, David found that the king used both his wife and friend in attempts to capture and kill him. Even though Saul acted irrationally and unjustly toward his loyal servant, David committed to never retaliate or take vengeance into his own hands.

On at least two occasions, David had opportunity to take Saul's life and ascend to his throne. Once, when Saul had pursued him into the wilderness, David happened upon Saul in a cave. He stealthily slipped behind the king and cut off a strip of his garment. On another occasion, he happened upon him and his bodyguards as they all slept. This time he took his javelin (perhaps the same one that had been hurled at him previously) and his water bottle. Rather than taking his life, David simply took a token to prove to Saul that he actually had the king within his power. On both of these encounters, Saul was forced to acknowledge that David was acting righteously toward him, while he was acting out of unjustified anger.

When David was only a little shepherd boy, the prophet Samuel had anointed him as the next king of the nation. Even though he lived for many years with this promise from God burning in his heart, David knew that it was not his place to try to take the throne by climbing the corporate ladder, as we would say in our modern society. We think that to get up the ladder, we must pull down the one who is above us. David, on the other hand, had apparently learned early in life the principle that he later recorded in the book of Psalms, *Promotion cometh neither from the east, nor from the west, nor from the south, but God is the judge; He puts down one, and sets up another.* (verses 75:6-7) Even though, the Spirit of God had departed from Saul and had anointed him, David determined to continue to show total respect and loyalty to the man as long as he sat on the throne where God had originally placed him.

The next relationship that we must understand is how to deal with the people who are below us. This principle is illustrated in the lives of the men who came seeking refuge with David when he had to flee from the king's court. These men were described in the Bible as *every one who was in distress, every one who was in debt, and every one who was discontented.* (I Samuel 22:2) In our modern vernacular, they were riffraff, outcasts, ne'er-do-wells – in general, square pegs in a society made up of round holes. It is incredible what David did with these square pegs; he whittled them into shape so that they not only fit into society, but also actually stood out as superior to their peers. Chapter twenty-three of II Samuel recounts how this band of riffraff became notable warriors who accomplished feats of strength, valor, and cunning that would easily win them recognition by Guinness and Ripley. Unlike the contemporary philosophy that I look tall when everyone around me is small, David knew that it was his responsibility to help those under him to become all they could be. As he tried to pull them up the ladder, he had to step up to the next rung himself. Without focusing on climbing the corporate ladder, he found himself getting closer and closer to the top each time he tried to help those under him achieve.

David's relationship with Jonathan illustrates the relationship we must develop with those who are beside us – our peers. Jonathan and David were apparently about the same age, they were both accomplished warriors; and it seems that they shared many of the same interests. There was, however, one possible bone of contention between them: Jonathan, who was captain over one third of the army while Saul's two other sons were not given positions of leadership (I Samuel 13:2, I Chronicles 10:6), was the heir apparent for the throne while David was the one anointed by the prophet to ascend to the royal seat – these two young men could have seen each other as rivals rather than friends. David and Jonathan, however, determined to support rather than challenge each other. They both seemed to know that God would ultimately decide who would be the next to wear the crown and that there was no purpose in their contending with each other for it.

Too often, we fail to see our peers as conveyors of God's blessings; instead, we tend to see them as contenders for the blessings of the Lord. The story of two local pastors illustrates this point dramatically. One pastor had a very large, exploding congregation; the other had a small, struggling group of followers. When the pastor with the growing congregation was forced to relocate to a larger facility, he bought a plot of ground just a few blocks from the other pastor's church. As soon as the construction began, the pastor of the smaller church began to feel very threatened by the fact that the larger congregation was moving into his "turf." He was afraid that the larger church would swallow him up. When the new pastor learned of the other pastor's concerns, he graciously asked him out to lunch. He reached across the table and reassured the troubled pastor, "Please don't view me as an opponent. See me as a partner together with you on the same team doing the same task of bringing the gospel to this community. Every Sunday there are going to be thousands of people who will drive past your church on their way to visit my service. The thing you may not know is that when they get there, there will be hundreds who do not want to come back again. Some won't like my sermon; some won't like our music; some won't like worshiping in such a large group – but for one reason or another, they will not be happy at my church. Many of them will remember seeing your building as they came to mine and will decide to try visiting your service the next Sunday. And many of them will stay after they visit with you once." With this little pep talk, the young pastor won the older pastor's confidence and they became partners rather than opponents. The result was that, the smaller church doubled in size within the first year that the big new church was open! I always tell pastors and Bible college students to view other churches in the community as seedbeds. If someone from their church decides to move to another church, consider him as a seed planted into the other church's ministry. Claim God's promise of a multiplied harvest of thirty-, sixty-, or a hundred-fold increase on his membership and the tithes and offerings that he is now giving to the other church. Instantly, that other pastor will become an avenue of increase rather than a drain!

David also had winning relationships with his supporters, those who were behind him. We often use the expressions like, "I'm behind you all the way," or "I'm behind you on this one," to register our support of a person and his projects. In David's life, it was the ones who had started out under him who became the ones who were so powerfully behind him. One story from the chronicles of David's mighty men poignantly illustrates the relationship between the king and his men. In the heat of battle one day, David made one of those wistful comments we often make when we long for the better times we remember of the past, "If only I could have a drink of water from the well at Bethlehem!" I'm certain that any water would have served to slake his thirst, but his soul cried out for the cool, clean waters of the community well outside the village gates because of the association with the blissful days of his childhood when, as a shepherd, he would draw deeply from that well to refresh himself and his sheep. When his bodyguards heard his sigh, they secretly broke from their ranks and fought their way through the enemy lines to get to the well. Once they had filled their flasks with the precious water, they again fought their way through the thick of the battle to bring the offering to their commander and chief. When David was offered the flask, he was surprised that his men had risked their lives to push through the fray in order to satisfy his whimsical request. Awestruck by their bravery and sacrifice, he refused to drink but poured the water on the ground as a libation before the Lord. The key principle in this lesson is that he understood the love and dedication of his men as being inspired, not by him, but by the life of God they saw in him. Therefore, he presented the water as an offering to God – the one who really deserved it. For those who are behind us, we must learn to recognize that any good they are attracted to in us is not of ourselves, but of Christ who lives inside us.

In the same fashion that we have supporters behind us, we will likely have opponents in front of us – the "in your face" sort of people who challenge and accuse us. The classic example in David's life was Shimei who openly accosted and ridiculed David as he fled Jerusalem during the attack by his son Absalom. On what was already likely the most humiliating day of David's life, this rogue scoundrel made the most unthinkable spectacle of the king by chasing alongside him as he fled before the advancing army and slandered him publicly, calling him every nasty name imaginable. Later, when David returned to Jerusalem in triumph, Shimei came bowing before the king to apologize for his foolishness and unwarranted accusations. Although David's men wanted to kill him, David spared the culprit's life. The king knew that, just as his supporters favored the life of God they saw in him, it was the manifestation of God inside him that had stirred up a manifestation of the demonic forces within Shimei.

For those who affront us with an "in your face" challenge, we must learn to realize that they are not so much attacking us but are fighting the Spirit of God inside us. At that point, we must remember Ephesians 6:12, *For we wrestle not against flesh and blood, but against principalities, against powers, against the rulers of the darkness of this world, against spiritual wickedness in high places.* For these individuals, we must pray as Jesus did for those who drove the nails into His flesh, *Father, forgive them for they don't even know what they are doing.*

Chapter Six
Have a Heart

We have learned that David's key and the key we need to open the door for us to reach our world is to have a perfect heart. Of course, we've all heard the expression, "Have a heart," but let's consider exactly what that means. To get started, let's take a short trip to the lush tropical island of Sri Lanka, a palm-studded treasure of white sandy beaches and dense jungle dangling just off the coast of India, not far from the equator – a perfect place except for the fact that the island suffers from extreme poverty. It is into this tragic agony of human suffering that our guide Deo Miller, along with his wife Elaine, will lead us:

"When we stopped by the Sumith Feeding and Training Center, a delicious aroma filled the air as Elaine and I stepped from the van. Lunch, bought fresh every day by staff members, simmered in large kettles over propane burners. A meal for several hundred children required four to five hours of preparation time. Each vegetable simmered in a separate pot with onions, chili peppers, and curry added for taste. I smelled potatoes, leeks, carrots, and rice – the mainstay of their diet.

"Some of the younger children sat on the long benches, eating the meal with their fingers. Lunch was served at about two-thirty or three in the afternoon in the Sri Lankan custom. Children may take seconds or thirds as long as they do not waste food. A huge bowl of rice sat in the center of each plate. The curried fish, hard-boiled egg, and curried vegetables formed a circle around the rice. When finished, the children washed their own bowls and plates under the water tap and stacked them in a pile. After lunch, everyone gathered for religious training before going home for the day.

"We waved to the small children. They stopped eating long enough to smile and wave back. Then we walked into the mat-making room. I expected to be greeted by ten-year-old Surakata who is always eager to tell us about his progress on his rug mat project. However, he was not there. I asked the director, 'Do you know where Surakata is?' She shrugged her shoulders and replied, 'He might be sick, or maybe he's running errands for his mother.' Although we emphasize regular attendance, sometimes the parents do not understand the importance of a daily commitment to the program. If they need work done at home or help with the younger children, they ask the boy or girl to stay home for a day.

"About a week later, we returned to the Sumith Center. Surakata was still missing. The center leader said, 'Deo, we're worried now about Surakata. He attended regularly. It's not like him to be absent over a week. If I give you directions to his home, will you stop by this afternoon?' I nodded. Elaine and I climbed in the van and I instructed the driver who drove us through the lush jungle growing along the riverside. The narrow road wound back and forth, following the meandering river to the village where Surakata lived.

"The driver parked. I walked up the crooked trail leading to the village. A woman who was washing her clothes in the river directed me to the hut where Surakata lived. Surakata's mother sat outside the shanty. She rocked back and forth, tightly clutching her knees in her arms. A low moan escaped from her lips. Tears streamed down her cheeks.

"I walked up to her and placed my hand on her shoulder. 'Hello. I'm Deo Miller from the Sumith Center. We've missed Surakata. Where is he?' 'He's terribly sick' was the mother's tired response. 'I don't know what's wrong with him.' 'Where is he?' I repeated. 'He's lying inside on the floor,' she answered, motioning to the entrance of her home.

"I entered the hot, musty hut, bending down as I walked through the low doorway. When my eyes became adjusted to the dark interior, I saw Surakata curled up on a mat in the corner. His body was contorted into an unnatural position. I tried to speak to him, but he was unaware of my presence. His forehead burned with fever. I picked up the semiconscious boy, mat and all, and carried him out of the stifling hut. I laid him gently on the ground near his mother. He remained in the strange, fetal position, unable to move or communicate.

"'How long has he been like this?' I asked. 'Almost a week. I can't break the fever.' The mother's penetrating eyes searched mine for reassurance. She asked, 'Will Surakata die?' I could not meet her gaze. Instead, I stared in horror at the distorted figure before me. 'I'll take him to the hospital. I have a car here. Do you have a blanket that I can wrap him in?' The woman entered her house and returned with a tattered piece of fabric. I wrapped the frail body and gently lifted Surakata into my arms. Carefully I hiked down the winding path to the van.

"When the driver saw the seriousness of the situation, he gunned the engine, winding us through the traffic in our makeshift ambulance. A nurse greeted us at the emergency entrance of the large, white government hospital. Upon seeing the boy, she shook her head. 'No hope, no hope.' Ignoring her diagnosis, I signed the necessary forms to admit the gravely ill boy for treatment. Then, Elaine and I returned to our flat, leaving Surakata in the hands of God and the hospital staff.

"Six weeks later, the hospital released the young boy. I visited his home and emphasized the doctor's advice to his mother. 'Surakata can't fetch water from the river or carry firewood. Making him do heavy labor of any kind will kill him. His older sister can bring food home from the center for him each day.' His mother nodded and said, 'I promise to let him rest. My husband left us last year. It is difficult to get the chores done, but the other children can help. I want my son to live.'

"I stared at her, trying to phrase my next words. I knew Surakata had participated in the center's program for almost six months. 'When Surakata first became sick, why didn't you tell someone at the center? Why didn't you do something?' She looked guilty and hung her head. 'He was sick before, but he always got well. I gave him the herbs, but this time they didn't help. He burned up with fever. He got sicker.' 'We told you to come to the center whenever you have a problem. Why didn't you come?' The mother shook her head. Sickness was a way of life in her village. 'I didn't want to bother them. I thought the herbs would make him well.'

"Exasperation welled up in me as I watched the reaction of Surakata's mother. 'Why didn't you take him to the hospital? Why didn't you catch a bus to the government hospital? Treatment is free only a few miles away!' Her sad eyes met my gaze as she softly replied, 'I would have taken him, but I didn't have two rupees.' Suddenly I understood. The bus fare to the hospital was one rupee each way. Surakata almost died because his mother did not have eight cents for bus fare.

"Shortly after this incident we returned to the U.S. for a short visit. One day I stood on a street corner watching two boys buy ice cream cones. They each received a double-dipper cone and a dime in change. One of the dimes slipped out of the boy's hand and rolled under a parked car. He looked at his friend, shrugged his shoulders, and walked away. Retrieving the dime was not worth his effort. I thought of how Surakata almost died for the lack of eight cents. I wondered how many other children would die in poverty from a lack of bus fare to the hospital." (Adapted from You Start With One by Deo Miller)

Surakata's health, future, and even life depended upon less than a dime – an amount so small that many of us, like the boy at the ice cream stand, wouldn't even go to the trouble to pick it up from the street. To Surakata, those few cents could have made his life totally different. If only someone would have had a heart for him.

Before you respond with any guilt feelings about living in abundance while the world is full of Surakatas, let me tell you another little story. At a fundraiser banquet for a humanitarian organization, a businessman reached across the table to grab a roll out of the breadbasket. As he stretched his arm, his sleeve pulled up just enough to expose his expensive watch. One of the other guests at the table made a comment about how many hungry children could have been fed with the cost of the watch. The businessman responded by unashamedly telling how many families would be fed with the contribution that he had made that very evening. You see, life doesn't have to be an either/or decision; it can be – and in fact was designed to be – a both/and situation. Both the Old and New Testaments confirm that God's desire is to give us both seed to sow – resources to give away – and bread to eat – sufficiency for our own needs and desires. (Isaiah 55:10, II Corinthians 9:10) In other words, God is big enough to bless us while making us big enough to bless others.

Now that we've mentioned the banquet at which the businessman and the other guest got into a rather interesting conversation, let's just imagine what it would be like to have a really, really large banquet and invite not just your friends – but the whole world! Well, of course, it would be impossible to get all seven billion of the folks on planet Earth together at one place for one large meal. But let's suppose that we were to choose one hundred guests to come represent the rest who could not join us. If we did this, our banquet room would be filled with fifty-seven Asians, twenty-one Europeans, fourteen from the Americas, and eight Africans. More than half of the guests would be less than thirty-five years old. Less than one-third of them would be white. Only one person in the whole room would have a college education, and only seventy of those sitting down to the meal would be able to read the menu for the meal – assuming that it was made available in their languages.

Gazing over the room, we would notice a marked distinction among the guests. There would be six guests – all from the United States – who seem to be substantially better off than the rest. In fact, those six individuals would actually own more than all the rest of the diners combined. It would certainly be obvious from their appearance that at least eighty of our guests have grown up in substandard conditions including homes without proper heating and plumbing – or even without a home at all. A large portion of our guests would be sick – in fact, one will die before the meal is over. A number of the women – including many teenage girls – will be pregnant; and at least one will give birth while our dinner is being served.

But the most dramatic thing we will observe will be the reaction of the guests to the food and the service at this particular banquet. You see, at tonight's banquet we are going to serve each guest the same food he is accustomed to eating! At one table, we will find a few healthy, well-dress guests who are handed menus that look more like catalogs listing every kind of imaginable dish: fresh fruits, vegetables of every kind, pizza, hamburgers, seafood, roast beef, chicken, and steak. In addition, they are handed dessert menus from which to choose ice cream, cake, and pie. Yet, this isn't all! These guests have brought their dogs and cats with them, so a variety of pet foods is also offered. As those at this table enjoy their meals, they laugh and joke about needing to lose weight and find a good diet program – all the while, seeming oblivious to the rest of the guests. All throughout the meal, the waiters repeatedly return to their table with more and more servings. Finally, the table is heaped with more than the party could possibly eat. Still unaware of the others in the room, they instruct the server to rake the leftovers from the table into the trash.

Most of the rest of the tables are not handed a menu; the guests are simply offered whatever comes out of the kitchen – in most cases a simple plate of rice. Sometimes, beans or cooked vegetables are mixed in with the rice. Occasionally, some chicken or fish is blended in. Very rarely does any pork or beef appear with these dishes. Not only are these guests treated differently in what they are served, they are also served in a dramatically different way. Rather than having a large table with soft chairs and a waiter to care for their needs, they are crowded together around a simple table and told to serve themselves.

For the most part, there is sufficient food to go around, but about one-fifth of the total guest roster will arrive hungry – and leave hungry. In fact, at least eight of those present are suffering from chronic malnutrition. Some of these unfortunate guests are not even offered a place at the table, but are told that they are to dine on scraps that are dropped by the other guests. To them, an all-you-can eat buffet means a trash bin or a garbage dump. Even more rudely, they are barred from the scraps of the first table where as much was thrown away as was eaten; rather, they are forced to beg from the patrons who are barely being served enough for themselves.

As if these discriminations were not enough, we take one last survey of the banquet hall to notice that at least twenty of our guests have been served dirty glasses full of off-colored water with questionable items floating in it. Polluted and disease-contaminated as it is, that is all these guests are offered to slake their thirst.

Atrocious! Unthinkable! Unimaginable! Yes, it is. But it is also true. This is exactly the way the human family lives and eats each day. This is a picture of the world if it could be reduced to just one meal together.

The greatest horror of this banquet is that there is plenty of food available for everyone, yet most of the guests were not fed properly. The same is true about the real world: statistically, there is more than enough food to adequately feed the world's population. Even as the world's population explodes, the ability to produce food is expanding faster than the human family is growing. The truth is that world hunger is more of a distribution problem rather than a supply problem. If the world's food supply were properly dispersed, everyone on the planet could enjoy a delightful meal every day.

There are many reasons for food shortages in various parts of the world. In some places, it is drought; in some spots, it may be flood; in other areas, it may be earthquakes; in still other places, it may be hurricanes or other storm systems; occasionally, volcano eruptions or other natural traumas may be at fault. But in most of the world, deprivation comes from human-imposed shortages. Wars, ethnic cleansings, corrupt governments, and plain and simple greed have kept the needed supply of food out of the hands and mouths of the masses – resulting in human-induced famine.

The travel log of my first experience in the deteriorating Soviet Union just at the end of the Communist regime records my reaction as a member of the free world encountering the ravages of man-made hunger.

The shortage of goods was apparent everywhere. Outside every shop, we saw lines of at least thirty to forty people waiting their chance to buy goods. It was sad to see the little package each person was holding in his hand when exiting the shop after having waited so long to get in. In addition, each shop carried only one or two items, so the people had to wait in line after line to buy first meat, then milk, then bread, then eggs – all of which were rationed in unbelievably small quantities. Even in what could be considered a nice restaurant, we found that many items on the menu were simply not available and that the napkins had been cut into tiny squares so that one napkin could be stretched to service a full table of guests.

The depravity in the land was simply a result of political oppression, not from any natural disaster. Jesus told a parable that emphasized that our response to the hurting and hungry of the world is the yardstick by which He measures those who claim to be believers.

> *When the Son of man shall come in his glory,*
> *and all the holy angels with him, then shall*
> *he sit upon the throne of his glory: And*

before him shall be gathered all nations: and he shall separate them one from another, as a shepherd divideth his sheep from the goats: And he shall set the sheep on his right hand, but the goats on the left. Then shall the King say unto them on his right hand, Come, ye blessed of my Father, inherit the kingdom prepared for you from the foundation of the world: For I was an hungred, and ye gave me meat: I was thirsty, and ye gave me drink: I was a stranger, and ye took me in: Naked, and ye clothed me: I was sick, and ye visited me: I was in prison, and ye came unto me. Then shall the righteous answer him, saying, Lord, when saw we thee an hungred, and fed thee? or thirsty, and gave thee drink? When saw we thee a stranger, and took thee in? or naked, and clothed thee? Or when saw we thee sick, or in prison, and came unto thee? And the King shall answer and say unto them, Verily I say unto you, Inasmuch as ye have done it unto one of the least of these my brethren, ye have done it unto me. Then shall he say also unto them on the left hand, Depart from me, ye cursed, into everlasting fire, prepared for the devil and his angels: For I was an hungred, and ye gave me no meat: I was thirsty, and ye gave me no drink: I was a stranger, and ye took me not in: naked, and ye clothed me not: sick, and in prison, and ye visited me not. Then shall they also answer him, saying, Lord, when saw we thee an hungred, or athirst, or a stranger, or naked, or sick, or in prison, and did not minister unto thee? Then shall he answer them, saying, Verily I say unto you, Inasmuch as ye did it not to one of the least of these, ye did it not to me. And these shall go away into everlasting punishment: but the righteous into life eternal. (Matthew 25:31-46)

In another parable, Jesus illustrated the tragedy of lacking the heart to help the poor who show up at our worldwide banquet.

> *There was a certain rich man, which was clothed in purple and fine linen, and fared sumptuously every day: And there was a certain beggar named Lazarus, which was laid at his gate, full of sores, And desiring to be fed with the crumbs which fell from the rich man's table: moreover the dogs came and licked his sores. And it came to pass, that the beggar died, and was carried by the angels into Abraham's bosom: the rich man also died, and was buried; And in hell he lift up his eyes, being in torments, and seeth Abraham afar off, and Lazarus in his bosom. And he cried and said, Father Abraham, have mercy on me, and send Lazarus, that he may dip the tip of his finger in water, and cool my tongue; for I am tormented in this flame. But Abraham said, Son, remember that thou in thy lifetime receivedst thy good things, and likewise Lazarus evil things: but now he is comforted, and thou art tormented.*
> (Luke 16:19-25)

Let's think about the lesson we can learn from the parable of the separating of the sheep and goats and combine it with some points we've already discussed concerning David's heart attitude. Remember that we determined in a previous section of the book that his repentance prayer after committing adultery with Bathsheba was that he had sinned against God and God alone. (Psalm 51:4) Although David had violated a virtuous woman and killed an innocent man, he saw only God as his victim. The point that Jesus made in the parable is that when we do evil or good to even the least human, we have actually acted either for or against Him. We must learn to treat all men with the same love and respect that we would give to Jesus if we could physically encounter Him in each circumstance in life.

We speak of people who have a kind heart or those who have a hard heart. We sometimes say that we are disheartened or downhearted. When we are startled or enjoying a thrilling roller coaster ride, we might say that our heart leapt into our mouths. We often talk about people who have had a change of heart. Our physical hearts continue to beat every minute of our lives, pumping the life-giving blood throughout our bodies. In the same way, the heart of compassion must continue to beat throughout the year, not just around special holidays. We must have a heart for the world that is permanently transplanted into us. In the Bible, the prophet Ezekiel spoke of an emotional heart transplant by saying that God would take out a stony heart and replace it with a heart of flesh. This should be the objective of our concern as well – that we might have a new heart that is constantly caring for the hurting people around us and around the world.

Chapter Seven
We Haven't Gone Far Enough

My sister and I were enjoying a "fun day" in Atlanta when we decided to have lunch at a spot from our childhoods. We knew almost exactly where this particular drive-in was located, so we headed out to find it. Unfortunately, the city of Atlanta has grown a lot in the more-than-we-care-to-admit years since we were children, and the new modern buildings in the area fooled us into thinking that we had gone too far and had reached the downtown area. So we stopped, turned around, and retraced our route. Still, there was no drive-in, so we turned around again and made another attempt. Eventually, we decided that we must have miscalculated and kept driving even though we felt that we were too close to metropolitan Atlanta. And there, much to our chagrin, was the restaurant – just a couple blocks further down the road from the place where we had turned around several times. At that point, I suggested to my sister that, if we are ever looking for the place again, we will need to remember, "When you think that you've gone far enough, you haven't." Her immediate response was, "There's a sermon there somewhere." So here it is: Why haven't we gone far enough?

First, we haven't gone far enough because we have the wrong viewpoint of the material world. Jesus called it "little faith." We have faith, but our faith is in little things – not a big God. We look to the world around us for our needs – such as food, clothing, and protection – and even our emotional, social, and psychological support. Jesus addressed this problem in two different places with identical words, but within significantly different contexts.

> *Wherefore, if God so clothe the grass of the field, which to day is, and to morrow is cast into the oven, shall he not <u>much more</u> clothe you, O ye of little faith?* (Matthew 6:30)

This statement comes in context of the explanation in verse twenty-four that we serve riches, *No man can serve two masters: for either he will hate the one, and love the other; or else he will hold to the one, and despise the other. Ye cannot serve God and mammon.*

> *If then God so clothe the grass, which is to day in the field, and to morrow is cast into the oven; how much more will he clothe you, O ye of little faith?* (Luke 12:28)

This time the statement is made in the context of the rich farmer whom God called a fool because he trusted in his wealth. (verses 15-21) In this case, the implication is that we think that riches will serve us. Whether we think that we must serve riches or that they must serve us, we're still wrong! We must not serve this world nor be served by it. Instead, we need to see it in perspective of our God. This world and the riches in it are not nearly significant enough for us to serve, nor are they big enough to truly serve us.

> *Who hath measured the waters in the hollow of his hand, and meted out heaven with the span, and comprehended the dust of the earth in a measure, and weighed the mountains in scales, and the hills in a balance?* (Isaiah 40:12)
> *Behold, the nations are as a drop of a bucket, and are counted as the small dust of the balance: behold, he taketh up the isles as a very little thing.* (Isaiah 40:15)

The second reason we don't go far enough is that we have the wrong viewpoint of God. In Matthew 7:11, Jesus tried to give us the true perspective on our heavenly Father, *If ye then, being evil, know how to give good gifts unto your children, how much more shall your Father which is in heaven give good things to them that ask him?* All too often, we read parables like the story of the unjust judge in Luke chapter eighteen or the one of the unwilling neighbor in Luke chapter eleven through faulty filters that make us think that the stories are trying to tell us that we should view God as symbolized in these unsavory characters. The result of this viewpoint is that we feel that we have to beg and plead with God to get anything from Him. Certainly, the poor widow and the humiliated friend had to audaciously and shamelessly implore their resistant benefactors until they unwillingly granted their requests. However, these parables are not intended to teach us that God is nasty, stingy, grumpy, or lazy. Rather, they are intended to give us the black canvas of the worst of humanity as a backdrop upon which to paint the brilliant portrait of our heavenly Father who is more willing to bless us than we are desirous of receiving or even able to imagine. (Ephesians 3:20) Jesus wants us to understand that even the best of human fathers are still evil in comparison to our heavenly Father. If these evil human fathers know how to give us good gifts instead of booby prizes, what can we anticipate from our gracious, loving Father? We must stop comparing God to our own human standards of abusive fathers, deadbeat dads, or even caring fathers who simply can't afford to give their children good gifts. We have to erase our mental images of fathers who couldn't and those who wouldn't and replace them with a biblical view of our God.

> *For the eyes of the LORD run to and fro throughout the whole earth, to shew himself strong in the behalf of them whose heart is perfect toward him.* (II Chronicles 16:9)
> *For God so loved the world, that he gave his only begotten Son, that whosoever believeth in him should not perish, but have everlasting life.* (John 3:16)
> *He that spared not his own Son, but delivered him up for us all, how shall he not with him also freely give us all things?* (Romans 8:32)
> *It shall come to pass, that before they call, I will answer; and while they are yet speaking,*

I will hear. (Isaiah 65:24)
Your Father knoweth what things ye have need of, before ye ask him. (Matthew 6:8)

The third reason we don't go far enough is that we have a wrong perception of what we need.

If ye then, being evil, know how to give good gifts unto your children: how much more shall your heavenly Father give the Holy Spirit to them that ask him? (Luke 11:13)

We think that we need things when what we need is God and His kingdom. Matthew 6:33 tells us that if we will seek God's kingdom, everything else will come automatically. The problem we have is the old cart-before-the-horse scenario. We're looking for physical solutions when God is trying to get us to focus on the spiritual dimension first and wait for the physical to manifest as fruit of the spiritual root. I told an audience in Africa, who were concerned because their highway system was little more than enough asphalt to hold the potholes together, that they needed to pray for God's kingdom to be manifest in their country. When that happens, corruption will go – and so will the potholes.

The next reason we don't go far enough is that we have a wrong viewpoint about ourselves. Luke 12:24 tells us, *Consider the ravens: for they neither sow nor reap; which neither have storehouse nor barn; and God feedeth them: how much more are ye better than the fowls?* No matter how bad things get, we often have a hard time believing that we deserve any better. The parable of the prodigal son (Luke 15:11-32) gives us some great insights into this dilemma. The younger son, after having wasted his inheritance, came back to the father asking to be a servant. It was the only logical position for him since he had reneged on his responsibility to the family enterprise, essentially considered his father as dead by asking for his inheritance ahead of time, shamed the family name through his lifestyle, and wasted all that was his. Why should

142

he expect anything better? After all, he was no longer the son to a man he considered dead, and there was nothing left of his portion of the family wealth; anything that would come to him would have to be earned or else taken from the older brother's share. On the other end of the spectrum, we can see that the older brother had a mentality that was just as faulty. When he complained that the father had never given him a kid so he could have a barbeque with his friends, he was expressing a poverty mentality even though he was living right in the midst of the abundance of the family's wealth. All he could see was the duties and responsibilities that came with the family business; he could not see himself as enjoying any of the privileges and benefits. Certainly, he must have envisioned the day when the father would pass away and leave him the ranch, but in the meantime he had only a slightly higher perspective than that of his younger sibling. Rather than seeing himself as a hired hand, he saw himself as a manager; yet he still saw himself as an outsider to the blessings. Whether we stray or stay isn't the problem. The issue is whether we see ourselves as sons.

The fifth reason we don't go far enough is that we have a wrong viewpoint about our salvation.

> _Much_ _more_ then, being now justified by his blood, we shall be saved from wrath through him. For if, when we were enemies, we were reconciled to God by the death of his Son, _much_ _more_, being reconciled, we shall be saved by his life...But not as the offence, so also is the free gift. For if through the offence of one many be dead, _much_ _more_ the grace of God, and the gift by grace, which is by one man, Jesus Christ, hath abounded unto many...For if by one man's offence death reigned by one; _much_ _more_ they which receive abundance of grace and of the gift of righteousness shall reign in life by one, Jesus Christ...Moreover the law entered, that the

offence might abound. But where sin abounded, grace did much more abound. (Romans 5:9, 10, 15, 17, 20)
How much more shall the blood of Christ, who through the eternal Spirit offered himself without spot to God, purge your conscience from dead works to serve the living God? (Hebrews 9:14)

I almost fell out of my chair when a prominent Christian leader requested a particular song to be sung at his meeting, stating that it was one of his favorites. The song he wanted is based around the idea that Jesus could have saved the whole world with just one drop of His blood, yet He loved us so much that He went through the entire crucifixion. The thing that surprised me was that the minister has such a powerful comprehension of the gospel that it seemed incomprehensible that he could possibly have overlooked the glaring theological error at the song's foundation.

First of all, the very fact that Jesus agonized in the Garden of Gethsemane for three hours begging the Father for an alternative to the cross should have been enough clue that just one drop would not have settled the score. If just one drop was all that was needed, the Father would certainly have responded immediately that all Jesus needed to do was stop by the local clinic and have the nurse prick His finger and draw a quick sample. More importantly, the whole theological issue of the crucifixion is based on the fact that Jesus came to fulfill the Law. (Matthew 5:17) Certainly, Jesus fulfilled the Law by living a righteous life that measured up to each of the Law's requirements; however, there was another side to His need to fulfill the Law – that of fulfilling all the judgments of the Law. Since Jesus actually took upon Himself all the sins of the world (II Corinthians 5:21), He had to also bear the punishment associated with each and every sin listed in the Law. The Old Testament Law listed many forms of chastisement, including burning with fire, stoning, hanging, striking with a sword, scourging, and cutting off one's hand. Anything less than the full brunt of the crucifixion would not have satisfied the need to totally fulfill the Law. Jesus was paying for every sin, sickness, injury, and injustice in the history of the human race – every rape, every murder, every abduction for human trafficking, every mutilation by warlords, every drug dealer's entrapment – and it took the price He paid to cover the bill.

Yes, He paid the full price. But before we leave the topic with simply that, we need to consider another story. This one has to do with an old farmer who has gone to the bank to cash a check. The teller whipped out his cash and shoved it under the grate at the window, but the aged gentleman didn't just take the wad of cash and walk away as she expected. Instead, he slowly and deliberately counted each bill and totaled all the coins. As the teller watched the folks in line behind him begin to fidget, she asked if she had given him the correct amount. In his slow farmer's drawl, he responded, "Just barely." Although I've heard this story used to explain that it did take the full torture of the cross to settle our sin debt, I want to quickly point out that there is just as big a flaw in this story as in the song about the singular drop of blood. It is true that if Jesus had given anything less, it would not have been enough; however, when he did pay, He lavished His blessing on us. If I only have $9.99, I can't buy a $10 item. But if I have a million dollar check, I can pay for the $10 item and anything else I want. That's what Jesus did for us – He paid the full liability against us but also left a deposit on our account to cover far more than we can ever expend!

> *I am come that they might have life, and that they might have it more abundantly.* (John 10:10)
> *He that spared not his own Son, but delivered him up for us all, how shall he not with him also freely give us all things?* (Romans 8:32)

The next reason we don't go far enough is that we have a wrong viewpoint about our covenant position and possession.

For if the ministration of condemnation be glory, much more doth the ministration of righteousness exceed in glory...For if that which is done away was glorious, much more that which remaineth is glorious. (II Corinthians 3:9, 11)

These passages speak of the glorious experience of Moses' visitation with God on Mount Sinai. When he came back to the camp, the people demanded that he cover his face with a veil because the glow of the anointing was so strong that they couldn't stand to look at him. Think about the point that Paul is trying to get across here: the Old Testament law was so spectacular that Moses had to put a veil over his face to mitigate the shining light, but we don't recognize that what we have is even better than that. If the Old Testament covenant could give the multitude manna to eat for forty years, provide enough quail to give them protein for four decades, open the Red Sea, raise a dead man by simply touching a prophet's bones, make the sun and moon stand still, and kill giants – just imagine what untapped blessings are available in our better New Testament covenant!

Another reason we don't go far enough is that we have a wrong viewpoint about our prophetic place in the world. In I Corinthians 6:3, Paul wrote, *Know ye not that we shall judge angels? how much more things that pertain to this life?* Wow! What a revelation. Somehow, some day – we will be responsible for judging angels! Moreover – since God has entrusted such a significant position to us, we need to take responsibility for the lesser obligations He has left in our charge. But because we don't understand the awesome authority of our decisions and words, we think that what we say and do doesn't make a difference. On the contrary, our words and deeds are actually passing verdict on the world. One loving act of acceptance or word of kindness can actually change someone's course in life and determine his eternal destiny; on the other hand, one thoughtless – or even intentional – act of condemnation or cruel word of rejection can seal his fate and doom him for eternity. That's why we are held accountable for every idle word. (Matthew 12:36)

> *If any man see his brother sin a sin which is not unto death, he shall ask, and he shall give him life for them that sin not unto death. There is a sin unto death: I do not say that he shall pray for it.* (I John 5:16)
> *Whose soever sins ye remit, they are remitted unto them; and whose soever sins ye retain, they are retained.* (John 20:23)

One final area that I would like to discuss as to why we don't go far enough is that we have a wrong viewpoint of God's end-time plan.

> *Now if the fall of them* [the Jews] *be the riches of the world, and the diminishing of them the riches of the Gentiles; how* much more *their fulness?... For if thou wert cut out of the olive tree which is wild by nature, and wert graffed contrary to nature into a good olive tree: how* much more *shall these, which be the natural branches, be graffed into their own olive tree?* (Romans 11:12, 24)

Israel is God's chosen people. When they are in position, history is made. When a Joseph, an Esther, or a Solomon rises up, things change. Today, the Jewish people constitute about one fifth of one percent of the world's population, but they hold one out of every five Nobel Peace prizes. Just think what will happen when the whole nation of Israel is saved (Romans 11:26) and they are grafted back into their rightful position of authority in the earth!

Once we begin to realize how much more God has in store for us, the only questions left to ask are, "How much more do I want?" and "How far will I go with it?" Today, we stand at the interfaces of destiny. Let's go through the open doors, anticipating the provisions of the open windows of heaven as we take back the gates of hell.

I'd like to conclude this challenge with the words of the great apostolic prayer that Paul entreated over his dear brothers and sisters in Ephesus:

> *That the God of our Lord Jesus Christ, the Father of glory, may give unto you the spirit of wisdom and revelation in the knowledge of him: The eyes of your understanding being enlightened; that ye may know what is the hope of his calling, and what the riches of the glory of his inheritance in the saints, And what is the exceeding greatness of his power to us-ward who believe, according to the working of his mighty power, Which he wrought in Christ, when he raised him from the dead, and set him at his own right hand in the heavenly places, Far above all principality, and power, and might, and dominion, and every name that is named, not only in this world, but also in that which is to come: And hath put all things under his feet, and gave him to be the head over all things to the church, Which is his body, the fulness of him that filleth all in all.* (Ephesians 1:17-23)

Teach All Nations Mission

Teach All Nations Mission (TAN) is a global evangelical educational ministry birthed from the teaching ministries of Delron and Peggy Shirley. The name for Teach All Nations Mission was chosen to carefully indicate the exact heart of the Shirleys' mission. TAN's commitment is to establish a solid biblical foundation in national pastors and leaders so they can help enrich their own people. This vision is being accomplished by holding national leadership conferences and publishing and distributing Christian teaching materials in English and their local languages.

Someone accurately observed concerning the revival that is occurring in many parts of our world today that it is a mile wide but only an inch deep – the result of energetic evangelism by both missionaries and local Christians. Sadly, there is a marked shortage of teachers who are taking the next step in fulfilling our Lord's directive to teach them how to observe all that He has commanded. Therefore, Teach All Nations Mission has literally taken the words of Christ from Matthew 28:19, "Teach all nations," as its motto and mission statement.

TAN's commitment is to deepen that revival by training the pastors and leaders who then go back and strengthen their congregations. TAN pays for the travel and lodging of handpicked leaders because Delron and Peggy want to invest into their lives but know that these third-world saints could never afford to come at their own expense. TAN always provides the meals for all the guests during these conferences. The ministry also furnishes solid Christian literature in their local language or in English for those who understand the language.

Delron and Peggy realize that the challenge is much bigger than what they can accomplish in person; therefore, they have determined to expand the scope of their vision. One area of expansion includes a scholarship fund that will allow selected individuals to obtain a formal education in solid Christian colleges and Bible schools or through correspondence courses. The ministry has also assisted in building a Christian school in Zimbabwe and a Bible college in Nepal. Additionally, Teach All Nations assists the pastors and leaders they work with in times of need such as the tsunami in Sri Lanka, the earthquake in Nepal, and hurricanes in Belize and in the Turks and Caicos Islands. More recently, the ministry supported suffering Christians in twelve different nations who lost their source of income during the shutdowns during the COVID-19 pandemic.

Your gifts to and prayers for Teach All Nations will help the Shirleys continue their outreach to Christian leadership around the world.

Teach All Nations Mission
3210 Cathedral Spires
Colorado Springs, CO 80904
719-685-9999
www.teachallnationsmission.com
teachallnations@msn.com

Books by Delron & Peggy Shirley

Bingo, a Fresh Look at Grace
Christmas Thoughts
Cornerstones of Faith
Daily Bible Study Series (Five-Volume Set)
Daily Ditties from Delron's Desk
(Eight Volumes Available)
Doctor Livingstone, I Presume
Don't Leave Home Without It
Finally, My Brethren
Getting More UMPH out of Your Bible
Going Deeper in Jesus
The Great Commission – Doable
The IN Factors
In This Sign Conquer
Interface
Israel, Key to Human Destiny
The Last Enemy
Lessons Along the Way
Lessons from the Life of David
Living for the End Times
Maturing into the Full Stature of Jesus Christ
Maximum Impact
No Longer Bound
The Non-Conformer's Trilogy
Of Kings and Prophets
Passion for the Harvest
People Who Make A Difference
Positioned for Blessing and Power
Problem People of the Bible
Seeds and Harvest
The Seventh Man at the Well
So Send I You
So, You Wanna be a Preacher
Thirty-, Sixty-, One-Hundred-Fold
Tread Marks
Turning the World Upside Down and Back Again

Verse for the Day (Four Volumes Available)
Women for the Harvest
You'll be Darned to Heck
if You Don't Believe in Gosh
Your Home Can Survive in the 21ˢᵗ Century

Available at:
teachallnationsmission.com

www.ingramcontent.com/pod-product-compliance
Lightning Source LLC
LaVergne TN
LVHW051104080426
835508LV00019B/2051